Self-Evaluation and Psychotherapy in the Market System

Self-Evaluation and Psychotherapy in the Market System examines the ways in which the competitive, hierarchical nature of today's market system contributes to the issues that many clients bring to therapy. Instead of seeing a lack of self-esteem as the root of clients' problems, Glantz and Bernhard argue that self-evaluation—the struggle to achieve a high opinion of self—exacerbated by the market system, leads to stress and endless self-involvement. Beginning with an explanation of the connection between the market system and self-evaluation, this volume then goes on to describe an approach to therapeutic treatment designed to free clients from the negative effects of the market system by moving away from self-evaluation altogether. This is a must-read for therapists looking for a new approach to treating clients left questioning their place in a society that encourages competition and self-involvement.

Kalman Glantz, PhD, spent 28 years as a psychotherapist in private practice in Cambridge and Boston. He is the author of two previous books: *Exiles from Eden: Psychotherapy from an Evolutionary Perspective*, and, with J. Gary Bernhard, *Staying Human in the Organization.*

J. Gary Bernhard, EdD, has been involved in educational leadership for more than 40 years. He has previously served as director of the University Without Walls program at the University of Massachusetts Amherst.

Self-Evaluation and Psychotherapy in the Market System

Kalman Glantz and
J. Gary Bernhard

Routledge
Taylor & Francis Group
NEW YORK AND LONDON

First published 2018
by Routledge
711 Third Avenue, New York, NY 10017

and by Routledge
2 Park Square, Milton Park, Abingdon, Oxon, OX14 4RN

Routledge is an imprint of the Taylor & Francis Group, an informa business

© 2018 Taylor & Francis

The right of Kalman Glantz and J. Gary Bernhard to be identified as authors of this work has been asserted by them in accordance with sections 77 and 78 of the Copyright, Designs and Patents Act 1988.

All rights reserved. No part of this book may be reprinted or reproduced or utilised in any form or by any electronic, mechanical, or other means, now known or hereafter invented, including photocopying and recording, or in any information storage or retrieval system, without permission in writing from the publishers.

Trademark notice: Product or corporate names may be trademarks or registered trademarks, and are used only for identification and explanation without intent to infringe.

Library of Congress Cataloging-in-Publication Data
Names: Glantz, Kalman, author. | Bernhard, J. Gary, 1946– author.
Title: Self-evaluation and psychotherapy in the market system / by Kalman Glantz and J. Gary Bernhard.
Description: New York : Routledge, 2018. | Includes bibliographical references.
Identifiers: LCCN 2017057738 (print) | LCCN 2018005291 (ebook) | ISBN 9781351124966 (eBook) | ISBN 9780815355335 (hardback) | ISBN 9781351124966 (ebk)
Subjects: LCSH: Psychotherapy—Marketing. | Self-evaluation.
Classification: LCC RC465.5 (ebook) | LCC RC465.5 .G535 2018 (print) | DDC 616.89/14—dc23
LC record available at https://lccn.loc.gov/2017057738

ISBN: 978-0-8153-5533-5 (hbk)
ISBN: 978-1-351-12496-6 (ebk)

Typeset in Times New Roman
by Apex CoVantage, LLC

For Eva
Who made it possible

and

To JoAnn, Caitlin, and Amanda
I'm a lucky guy

Contents

	Introduction: Connections	1
1	Psychological Distress and the Market System	7
2	Ancient Emotions in a Strange New World	18
3	Children of the Market System	24
4	Work: Oppression or Opportunity?	30
5	Imaginary Sticks, Imaginary Stones: Undoing Self-Generated Distress	39
6	Farther Out? Some Additional Interventions	55
7	Some Sad Bedfellows of Self-Evaluation	61
8	A Little More on Anxiety	73
9	Self-Evaluation and Relationships	81
10	Illustrations from the Files	91
	References	105

Introduction
Connections

> It is not events that disturb people, it is their judgments concerning them.
>
> (Epictetus, *Discourses*)

Low self-esteem. Everyone knows it's bad. Every therapy targets it. But low self-esteem is only part of the problem. What kills joy and consumes life is the struggle to overcome it. It's the inner dialog, the argument about worth, the pressure to think highly of oneself. It's self-evaluation, the endless back and forth between a high opinion and a low opinion of one's value.

If you're stuck in low self-esteem, you're liable to be clinically depressed, but most people aren't stuck in it. They're on a mission to overcome it. It keeps coming back and they keep fighting it off by amassing evidence that would demolish it once and for all. But this mission is rarely successful; the negative self-representation keeps coming back and has to be dealt with anew. It's a medusa, a gorgon, a monster that can't be slain. The search for self-justification is often a form of self-torture.

After years of conversation, reading, and writing, we have come to the conclusion that the market system, whatever its glories, and there are many, tends to foster this kind of obsessive concern with the self and its position in an imaginary internal hierarchy.

Take Andrew, for example. He is a reasonably successful businessman. When he tries to define himself, he runs into trouble. When he realizes he is doing well, he almost immediately thinks he is doing much better than he deserves, so he looks around to see if anyone has figured out that he is a fraud. That possibility—that thought—makes him anxious and makes him think that other people must be doing better, which makes him depressed.

It took me some time to realize that this common condition was a regular, predictable product of the market system. The first time it hit me, I had a strange sensation made up of equal parts excitement and dread. Could it be that a single variable could be the key to so much psychological distress?

2   Introduction

Was there going to be a sort of common entry point to this distress? Or would this insight turn out to be just another one-size-fits-all theory of everything?

Over the years, as I used the cluster of interventions described in this book more extensively, the fear of being ridiculously grandiose subsided somewhat. I could see both the relevance and the limitations of the ideas, and I settled into comfort and contentment. Only when I started to write about my findings did the misgivings and doubts resurface.

I continue to be surprised. Psychological conditions and emotional distress make a different kind of sense when viewed through the lens of the economic system. Much of what is seen in the office of a therapist looks like a response, and a fairly obvious one, to characteristics of the American market system: excessive competition, individualism, ambition, acquisitiveness, and the reckless pursuit of efficiency. These social traits tend to deform identity, generating anxiety and provoking depression.

Entitlement and deprivation. Affluenza and despair. These descriptors of social conditions illuminate a good slice of individual pathology. Inequality and competition create a spectrum of social types, from epicures to addicts, and a series of pathological belief systems like "They're all against me" or "I've gotta just be out for myself." The social system explains much of what we see in our offices.

But why does the market system create these conditions? Why do the characteristics of the market system foster painful belief systems? In *Exiles From Eden: Psychotherapy From An Evolutionary Perspective*, one of us (Glantz) argued that a good deal of human distress derives from a mismatch between our genes and the current environment. Human beings evolved in small, hunter-gatherer bands—bands in which cooperation was an essential survival skill, not something people had a choice about. Everyone in the band was related to everyone else, and therefore everyone belonged— automatically. As a result, we humans carry, in our DNA, the need to belong to a group and an expectation of cooperation, fairness, and equality. The genes haven't changed much, if at all; the environment has, quite drastically.

With the development of agriculture and sedentary living, it became possible for individuals to achieve levels of wealth, status, and power that were unknown to our foraging ancestors. The result: social environments that don't match our biological needs and expectations.

In two books, *Staying Human in the Organization* and *Reuniting America*— the working title was "Saving the Market System"—Glantz and Gary Bernhard explored the effects of this mismatch and examined the rift between individual achievement and group cooperation. What we now realize is that the market system is a *particular* form of environment. Its interaction with our genes, which come down to us from those hunter-gatherer ancestors, produces particular forms of distress.

Introduction 3

Specifically, the market system fosters a particular form of identity—identity based on achievement rather than on belonging. The need for belonging urges us toward cooperation and inner peace. The overemphasis on achievement leads in the direction of competition and comparison. When identity is based on achievement and not on belonging, on self and *not* other, loneliness, desperate ambition, obsessive comparison, imaginary failure, perfectionism, and self-victimization are likely outcomes.

Basing identity on achievement tends to inflame self-evaluation. People take it for granted that they have to reach a judgment about themselves—in essence a rating. They spend their lives comparing themselves to others, usually negatively. This procedure keeps them busy. It can provide motivation of a sort—a desperate desire to avoid being stuck with a negative opinion of themselves. Here's a typical example:

Therapist: I was wondering about something. You've been pretty successful. Do you run any doubts about your competence?

Client: Sure, doesn't everybody?

Th: Can you tell me about them?

Cl: It's pretty normal. Whenever I come across someone who makes more money than me, or just someone who has achieved a lot, I ask myself: "Why don't I have that or why didn't I do that?"

Th: Really?

Cl: Yeah, I always compare myself to someone who is above me, never below. I don't know why I do that.

Even royalty is not exempt. Here's what Zoe Heller (2017) had to say about Prince Charles, heir apparent to the British throne, in a review of a biography by Sally Bedel Smith: "The strange artificiality of his youthful 'achievements,' and the nagging self-doubt it engendered, seems to have left him peculiarly vulnerable to the blandishments of advisers willing to reassure him." Prince Charles could, perhaps, have taken mental refuge in *belonging* to a royal family, but apparently even that wasn't enough.

Of course, self-evaluation—judgment about oneself—is not new. St. Augustine was constantly judging himself against what he believed god wanted of him; religious individuals have been doing it for hundreds of years.

Furthermore, self-evaluation is so common that it must derive from something useful. We suspect that it derives from *situational awareness*. It is useful to be aware of one's position in one's group. It is necessary, in a group-living species, for individuals to be aware of the opinions, attitudes, needs, and desires of others on a moment-to-moment basis. It is essential to be able to conform to group norms where one's survival depends on others.

4 *Introduction*

But when this ever-shifting situational awareness turns into fixed judgments about the worth of self, we get pathological self-evaluation. By rewarding competition and comparison, the market system manufactures pathological self-evaluation out of the raw material of situational awareness.

Relative Failure

The plight of the poor, the unemployed, and others at the bottom of the modern money hierarchy receives a lot of attention, but that isn't what this book is about. The people who come to the offices of psychotherapists are often materially successful. This book is about those clients. The problem that stalks them is *relative failure*. When they compare themselves to others they easily find someone who is doing better. Actually, all they have to do is watch some advertisements or read some Facebook posts. Comparative or relative failure is a prime source of negative self-evaluation.

Here's a typical example:

Cl: The pregnancy is costing a lot more than I thought it would. Insurance doesn't pay for all kinds of things. There's expenses with the baby coming on, Christmas presents for the family. And my car just died. We're trying to save for retirement too. It feels overwhelming.

Th: Yeah, you look really distressed.

Cl: We're so focused on the negative. I wish there was something positive to work on.

Th: What would that be like?

Cl: [struggling with tears] Don't know. I'm not happy, and I should be. I have a job, a wife that I love, a baby on the way, money in the bank, but I don't feel happy.

Th: Tell me, when you think about the money problems, do you have any thoughts about yourself?

Cl: I can't get it together. I can't handle it. I'm no good.

In a sense, therapy often colludes with self-evaluation. Therapists tend to believe in a hallowed principle—that the unexamined life is not worth living. But exploration—of the past, of behavior, and/or of thought patterns— can lead to more self-criticism, if the therapist is not on guard. When clients are encouraged to keep striving for a positive view of themselves, instead of being weaned from their addiction to self-evaluation, the risk is that they will remain immersed in themselves.

In *Stand Firm: Resisting the Self-Improvement Craze* (2017), Danish psychologist Svend Brinkmann put forward the idea that self-help books can actually make people feel worse. Such books, he argues, promote the idea

Introduction 5

that people should aim for constant self-improvement, a goal that people often fail at. Therapy that encourages people to immerse themselves in the analysis and perfection of the self may also be counterproductive.

But back to the market system. The market system didn't have an immaculate conception. It grew out of pre-existing politico-economic systems, especially the mercantilist system that horrified Adam Smith, the man generally credited with formulating the principles of the market system. Mercantilism, which functioned as the economic version of the divine right of kings and absolute monarchy, was strongly marked by hierarchy, inherited inequality of status, and centralization. A lot of the problems we attribute to the market system in this book predate it. But, unfortunately, these problems haven't disappeared from the market system and are sometimes exacerbated by it.

Nevertheless, what Adam Smith hoped, that the market system would emancipate the ordinary person, has come to pass, to a significant degree. So don't take this book as an attack on the market system or the American economy. There's a lot worse out there: despotism, oppression, police states, repression, mind control, terror, corruption, stagnation, starvation, and slavery, to name a few.

Furthermore, many people thrive in our system. They don't appear in the offices of psychotherapists and psychiatrists. This book is not about them. It's about the people who, for one reason or another, don't do so well psychologically.

All that competition and comparison leave some people with a chronically negative opinion of self. Those who chew the cud of imperfection tend to be miserable. To escape from the misery, they try to generate a positive opinion of self. This locks them into a permanent inner struggle, a struggle which results in oscillating self-representation, the inability to fix once and for all on an opinion of self.

Here's a typical example:

Th: You've told me that sometimes you are brimming with confidence and sometimes you're not. When you're not, how do you see yourself? Do you have a high opinion of yourself?

Cl: Of course not. I think I'm really terrible.

Th: But at other times, your opinion is different, right? You think you're actually very competent.

Cl: Right.

Th: Which do you think is right?

* * *

The first part of this book describes problems created by the current environment, seen in the light of the environment in which our species evolved.

6 *Introduction*

The final chapters describe a therapeutic approach that seeks to undo immersion in the vicissitudes of the self.

For the most part the work we have emphasized is cognitive; in order to exit from self-evaluation, the client has to recognize the relevant mental procedures and overcome them. However, many different techniques and tools can help in this process, including psychodynamic exploration of the past, meditation and relaxation techniques, couples work, hypnotherapy, etc. All these techniques and tools have been well-described by others so we will not be describing them.

This book doesn't pretend to deal with all the problems clinicians face. There are, of course, genetic differences between humans. A number of problems derive from those differences; one thinks of schizophrenia, the bipolar disorders, some personality disorders, OCD, and certain other forms of mental illness. Childhood sexual and physical abuse, which are hardly specific to any socio-economic system, will also remain largely outside the scope of this book.

The authors are well aware that almost any condition can be interpreted and dealt with in more than one way. Freud, for example, saw behavior emerging from roots in treacherous, subterranean chambers. Cognitive behaviorists, with their painstaking work-sheets, don't seem to pay much attention to social context. We think the influence of the market system, while perhaps not *the* royal road to the unconscious, is without doubt a major highway to the deeper levels of the psyche.

1 Psychological Distress and the Market System

The Market System

The market system is a way of organizing economic activity that leaves individuals and companies free to produce whatever they want, and free to sell what they produce at any price they can get. It is a method of organizing an economy that does not rely on planning by a central authority such as a government. Competition between sellers is supposed to keep prices down and direct production to products and services that people want. "The market," that is, the totality of buyers and sellers, makes the important economic decisions, not any person or institution. The market system is usually contrasted to socialism and communism, but is also fundamentally different from feudalism, fascism, and other forms of authoritarian control.

Books about the effect of the market system on human psychology, morality, and social relations tend to be negative. Psychoanalyst Paul Verhaeghe's book *What About Me: The Struggle for Identity in a Market-Based Society* (2014) is a typical example. Verhaeghe sees "neo-liberalism" and the market system as the source of all evil; politics, universities, unions, hospitals, information technology—everyone and everything has been tainted. But this view isn't useful for psychotherapists, who have to deal with all kinds of people. Some clients list to the left and some lean to the right. Psychotherapy is not—nor should it be—a political seminar, which is why our book seeks to present a balanced view of the system.

The Power and the Glory

Most people don't realize it, but the most important function of the market system has always been to protect people from despotism. Since the discovery of agriculture, sometime between 12,000 and 10,000 years ago, despots have ruled the earth. Government was created to rule and rulers have understandably ruled in their own interests. They have, often mercilessly,

8   *Psychological Distress and the Market System*

exploited those they ruled. They have taxed to death and tortured to death their unhappy subjects. And they invented war to increase their power, their territory, and their wealth.

The market system, which was first formulated by Adam Smith in the 18th century, is one of the few mechanisms ever devised that actually limits the power of government. As we said before, in a pure market system, individuals, not government, run the economy. The laws of economics, notably supply, demand, and competition, regulate it. Decisions by individuals, made in their own interests, replace the centralized decision-making that is the province of government. As a result, there are sources of power in society that do not stem from government and are not subject to the whims of rulers or ruling classes. This triumphant headline from the *Wall Street Journal* tells it all: "Microsoft Wins Fight With U.S." (July 15, 2016).

It has not escaped our notice that in the real world today, corporations have themselves accumulated too much power. Clearly the growth of corporate power is a major problem and we will discuss it later. But what happens when private sources of wealth and power don't exist? Well, that's largely the story of civilization. A central authority runs everything and rulers have no constraints.

Freedom and Wealth

Because it frees people to pursue their own hopes and dreams, the market system releases vast amounts of individual effort, energy, and creativity. This fosters technological change, which tends to bring material progress in its wake.

When transferred from the west to what was once called the Third World, the market system brought tens of millions of people out of poverty. India, China, and other Asian countries have been transformed. Back in the 1970s, India, under Indira Gandhi, was mired in admiration for the Soviet Union and the socialist dream. A traveler to India at that time found hopelessness and mind-numbing poverty. People were sleeping on the streets while large rats bounded over them; rickshaw-wallahs were eating dinner made of uncooked flour mixed with water they scooped from gutters. There are still horribly poor people in India today, but fewer by far. The freedom generated by the market system passed this way and is still working its magic.

Freedom and Mindset

The coming of the market system did more than bring people out of poverty; it changed the way they thought. In *The End of Karma* (2016), Somini Sengupta, writing about a psychic shift in India, was blown away by the

Psychological Distress and the Market System 9

explosion of ambition and ingenuity that followed the market-oriented reforms that began in 1991:

> The opening of the Indian economy went hand in hand with something far less tangible. . . . India is being propelled from within by what I regard as its most transformative generation—those who have grown up since economic reforms began in 1991. Their demands are reshaping the country (p. 9).

Hope now walks the streets of India. Even the lowest castes, who previously accepted their lot as a matter of karma, have begun to believe that they can influence their destiny. For example, a landless woman from the Arundhatiyaar community, the lowest among the lowest castes in Tamil Nadu State, became the first woman from her caste to run for presidency of her local governing body. "I came to this village 20 years ago," she declared,

> to live with my husband after we were married. Since then, I have never seen anyone from here running for the Panchayat president's election—everyone is afraid of upper caste landlords who hold most of the land here.
> (Upadhayaya, 2013)

She did not win the election, but she did inspire others in her community.

In the 1970s the Chinese were being starved and slaughtered by Mao and his communist cronies in government. Five-year plans paraded past each other in time, duly accompanied by misery. The Chinese still haven't mastered the market system—the state keeps screwing it up—but the fragments of free enterprise that their government tolerates have brought many of their millions to prosperity—as the wave of Asian tourists attests.

The Underside of the System

Poverty and Inequality

Alongside its glories, the market system has some well-known drawbacks. The most obvious: an inability to eliminate poverty. "Poverty" is relatively new in human evolutionary history. According to anthropologists who have studied the foraging way of life (e.g. Sahlins, 1968; Lee and Devore, 1976; Marshall Thomas, 1959; Shostak, 1981; Turnbull, 1961; Balikci, 1970), poverty as we know it didn't exist in the hunter-gatherer world. The foraging peoples didn't know wealth. They didn't "own" and they hardly possessed. They shared what they had, even if they did it grudgingly some of the time. Since our genes were formed in the hunter-gatherer world, most

10 *Psychological Distress and the Market System*

humans aren't comfortable with poverty, even when it afflicts other people. But poverty is an objective, material condition, not solely a mental misery. Unfortunately, there is no psychotherapy for poverty, so we will not be dealing with it in this book.

Inequality is another story. Inequality is a matter of perception and comparison. To register inequality, one has to perceive that someone has more or that someone has less, and then react to the difference. Inequality, therefore, is largely in the mind.

Inequality is not equally painful everywhere. In some cultures, people don't think they are responsible for having less than others. Inequality is seen as the result of a divine plan. But in a market system, where individuals are free to pursue their own interests and are held responsible for their fate, inequality can appear as proof of inadequacy and a sign of failure: "If people are free to do well and I'm not doing as well as that other guy, it must be my fault."

Unfortunately, inequality is inherent in the market system. If people are free to pursue their own interests, the outcome will not be equal. The only way to *eliminate* inequality is to have government set everyone's income, which would put everyone right back under the thumb of a central authority.

Abundance, Inequality, and Obesity

It may seem strange to treat abundance as a problem, but too much of a good thing can be deadly. Abundance didn't exist in our ancestral environment so many of us don't have genes that protect against it, as obesity and its panorama of diseases reveal. The market system, fortunately and unfortunately, is an engine of abundance.

Humans are not designed to turn down food. For our hunter-gatherer ancestors, who have bequeathed to us so many of their genes, food was hard to come by and getting it involved significant physical effort. There were no obese hunter-gatherers. Agriculture required even harder work. But the market system has made it possible for people to eat, well, like geese being fattened for the slaughter—the slaughter of heart disease, diabetes, and the like. It's the success of the system that gives us virtually unlimited access to the foods we can't turn down.

The problems don't affect everyone equally. Sugary cereals and drinks, starchy snacks, and fatty, salt-heavy meats cost less than healthier alternatives and are therefore attractive to people with low incomes. The prevalence of these foods, which are filling in the short term but lethal in the long one, results from the competition between companies for the consumer dollar. These companies and their foods are having a profound effect on human behavior and health.

Psychological Distress and the Market System 11

The Merging of Money and Status

Humans have always desired status and recognition, but in some societies, they gained it by "doing for" other people. In foraging societies, for example, good hunters acquired status because everyone in the group benefited from the kill. In the market system, people can get status by getting rich, whether or not the wealth proves useful to anyone else. This encourages the pursuit of activities which don't benefit the community.

Status is only useful to the community if it is the payoff to good works; when you can get it without the good works, the common good suffers. Rich people often do add to their status through charity, which restores status to its previous role, but charity is not obligatory, as the difference between Donald Trump and Bill Gates testifies.

Competitiveness

The study of evolution has made it clear that some degree of competition is inherent in life. Organisms are designed to seek their own survival, which sometimes brings them into conflict with other organisms. Humans are no exception; competition is inherent in human interaction. But the American market system glorifies it and offers winners supersized rewards.

Individuals with strong competitive impulses and significant levels of ability tend to thrive in this environment. But those who don't thrive tend to feel defeated. And since "success" is relative, even apparently successful individuals may think of themselves as losers if they don't think they are as successful as they "should" be.

The result is often depression, a toxic mix of shame, blame, regret, and hopelessness. Anxiety often accompanies the depression. People who feel defeated tend to have doubts about their ability to cope. They tend to imagine a future composed solely of disasters.

Instances of satisfying cooperation are relatively hard to come by in this system. To be sure, cooperation can be found in private, personal, and family life. But currently these cooperative experiences often don't carry as much weight as economic success. The human need to belong and to participate with others in the pursuit of common goals is rarely satisfied by working together in factories or corporations.

The Inevitability of "Failure"

Infinite opportunity makes failure almost inevitable. Not absolute failure, like homelessness or hunger, but, as we mentioned in the Introduction, failure by comparison or relative failure. Take the case of David Foster

12 *Psychological Distress and the Market System*

Wallace, the author of *Infinite Jest* (1996). He was acclaimed as one of the most innovative writers of his generation. He was married and had a good job, teaching at a college in California. It wasn't enough. He hanged himself.

From childhood on, writes David Kessler, author of *Capture: Unraveling the Mystery of Mental Suffering* (2016), Wallace didn't want to be ordinary. He wanted to be special. "Yet, as soon as he succeeded . . . he grew uneasy and then despairing. He wanted to be a good person but suspected something crooked about the way he had achieved success. . . . Contradictory impulses—yearning for greatness yet feeling like a fake with every new achievement—pushed him further into himself" (p. 4).

Kessler quotes Wallace as having scrawled somewhere: "Grandiosity—the constant need to be, and be seen as, a superstar." Grandiosity is, of course, the other side of the "worthless" coin. They both are what we have called pathologies of self-evaluation. These pathologies weren't born of the market system but they flourish there.

Perceived Uselessness

Many Americans suffer from the thought that they have no influence and no importance. To be fair, this perceived uselessness may be more a function of size than of the market system as such. But the market system produces size as it produces wealth. Too big to fail is bad for society; just plain *TOO BIG* is bad for individuals. It makes many feel too small to succeed. In vulnerable individuals, this feeling easily breeds a sense of futility that can bleed over into depression.

The Payoff to Selfishness

The *prisoner's dilemma* is a game that purports to show under what conditions two rational individuals might choose to cooperate or not to cooperate. Here's a standard version of the game:

Joe and Ken, two members of a criminal gang, are arrested and put in jail. Each prisoner is put in solitary confinement and has no means of communicating with the other. The prosecutors don't have enough evidence to convict the pair. In an effort to prevent them from going free, they offer each prisoner a choice: Betray the other by accusing him of committing the crime, or remain silent. The payoffs are as follows:

> If Joe and Ken each betray the other, each of them gets two years.
> If Joe betrays Ken but Ken remains silent, Joe will go free and Ken will serve three years.

Psychological Distress and the Market System 13

> Likewise, if Ken betrays Joe but Joe stays silent, Ken will go free and Joe will get three years.
>
> If Joe and Ken both remain silent, both of them will only serve one year in prison.

Clearly, the best bet would be to remain silent, but that would be risky; if one gang member remained silent while the other ratted, the guy who remained silent would get three years. The game is generally analyzed with these standard payoffs to what is called defection and cooperation.

The market system can be seen as one big prisoner's dilemma game. People constantly have to make choices, choices between self and other. But the payoffs are far from standard. The *payoffs to defection* are huge. Individuals can become incredibly wealthy by abandoning family and betraying friends; corporations can reap unimaginable profits by polluting the environment or otherwise violating the common good. In this way, people are frequently induced to behave in ways that are emotionally damaging. For example, Exxon scientists warned Exxon executives about global warming in the early 1980s, but the executives suppressed the results of the studies. In pursuing their own interests, they acted against the interests of the community. No one measures the psychological impact of such decisions on the people who make them.

Market Metastasis

A market economy is one thing. A market society is quite another. Here are a few ways market-system thinking has crept into other aspects of life.

Failure of Work-Life Balance

Hunter-gatherers didn't have to strive for work-life balance. For them, work was life and life was work. They hunted and gathered when they were hungry. They built shelters when they were hot, or cold, or otherwise inconvenienced by the weather. They didn't sacrifice the present for future gain because they knew no way to do that; investment hadn't been invented. Work-life balance was inherent in the system.

In the market system, people have to invent their own work-life balance. The failure to achieve it may be the most common mental health issue in our society. The difficulty of the task is perhaps where the market system impinges most obviously on mental health. The struggle *involves* just about everybody; it *engulfs* some.

Can you believe it? Many people choose (getting more) money over health and life! Why do people do it? Many reasons. The material rewards

14 *Psychological Distress and the Market System*

are virtually irresistible. Money is like sugar; we don't have a built-in genetic stop sign for it. "The more the merrier" is its mantra. And its fatal attraction. Furthermore, comparison with others is hard to escape and the envy of others is delightful. Finally, the thought of being labeled a failure, relative as failure might be, can drive people to ultimately self-injurious decisions.

Market-Guided Parenting

Recently, market-type thinking has taken on parenting. Do you feel powerless as a parent? Do you want to control your kids? Paul Raeburn and Kevin Zollman (2016) have a market-inspired solution.

If you have several kids, let them all bid on whatever they want to get. Suppose they want a chocolate malted. Hold an auction, but use chores as the currency. The one who is willing to do the most work gets the treat.

If you have only one kid, create a minimum bid—say, make your bed every day for a week. No more fighting, no more arguing, no more messy room, say the authors.

They go on to warn against using money as currency, because you as parent might weaken; you might feel sorry for the kid who overbid, or for the losers. You might be tempted to use the same amount of money to compensate the underprivileged. Lessons might be lost.

We don't know if this would work outside a lab, but is this the solution we want for parents who feel powerless? Do we want our kids to see every activity as a kind of commodity they have to compete for?

Dating and the High-Tech Lek[1]

Finding a mate has always been implicitly competitive; there are a limited number of appropriate partners, and these partners can choose someone else. But when marriages are arranged, or limited by tradition to specific categories, the competition is muted and may not even be experienced by the people involved.

The situation is different today. When individuals are completely responsible for finding their own mates, when they can choose among all the potential mates in the world, mating becomes overtly competitive. The Internet dating and mating sites have created a kind of high-tech *lek* where humans, both male and female, can display, like birds of paradise flaunting their feathers in the jungle clearings of Borneo. Today, it's hard to be satisfied with a good-enough spouse. Now people can compare themselves to the best and the beautiful. Now the results are public, which gives people another reason to blame themselves.

Psychological Distress and the Market System   15

In *Labor of Love: The Invention of Dating* (2016), Moira Weigel traces the beginning of what we now call dating to well-to-do students in the 1920s and 1930s. College men and women pursued one another with enough libidinous energy to foreshadow today's hook-up culture. The point wasn't to get married; it was to compete. Students rated one another. The higher you rated, the more you dated, and vice versa. Under these conditions, dating became more like a competitive game than a courtship ritual. The new mores led to greater freedom for men and women alike, but, says Weigel, the result "was a set-up that subjected girls to constant stress, self-blame and regret" (quoted in Schwartz, 2016, p. 79).

We've gone beyond the market economy; we've created a market *society*, where everything—dating, health care, education, the air, the water—is up for grabs. Many people can handle this kind of freedom, but some are manhandled by it.

Affluenza[2]

If there is any remaining doubt about the relevance of the market system to psychotherapy, consider affluenza, a condition which can be defined as a loss of determination, drive, and motivation due to unearned wealth—a not-uncommon feature of the market system. The client we shall call Arnold had a fairly typical case of it.

Arnold began missing therapy only a few weeks into it. But therapy wasn't the only thing he was missing. He hadn't been going to school either. He was waking up late, agonizing a bit, deciding it was too late, or simply not feeling like going, so he wouldn't. Once he had made that decision, he felt fine. He would start the day untroubled, doing things he liked. But then he would start feeling guilty: "I never accomplish anything."

Therapy forced him to think about this pattern. He didn't like what he was seeing, so he would get upset at the therapist: "I'm fine, I don't know why you're making a big deal out of it." They went around and around on it for some time, but without any success.

The therapist suddenly asked: "Are you going to inherit?" Arnold was taken aback. His first response was to get angry at the therapist for asking: "What's that got to do with therapy?!" Once he got over his shock and rage, the relevance became obvious. His father, a corporate lawyer, and his mother, an executive at a midsized corporation, had been paying for him to go to private schools for years. And, just as predictably, he had been dropping out. Arnold knew perfectly well that he would never have to make a living for himself. His good fortune had, at one and the same time, enraged him and sliced off his motivation.

War, Cooperation, and Community

Perhaps the crucial problem of the market system is its failure to prioritize community. Just how important cooperation and community are to psychological well-being is highlighted in *Tribe: On Homecoming and Belonging* (2016), Sebastian Junger's account of soldiers at war and afterward.

It seems strange, but many soldiers miss war after it's over. Part of the trauma of war seems to be giving it up. "For the first time in our lives," said one ex-soldier, "we were in a tribal sort of situation where we could help each other without fear. . . . You had 15 guys who for the first time in their lives were not living in a competitive society. . . . It was the absence of competition and boundaries and all those phony standards that created the thing I loved about the army" (p. 91).

A modern soldier returning from a war goes from the kind of close-knit group that humans evolved in—the foraging band—back into a society where most people work outside the home, children are educated by strangers, families are isolated from wider communities, and personal gain almost completely eclipses collective good. So even if soldiers come back to a family, they don't necessarily reenter a group that shares resources and experiences life communally. According to Junger, lack of social support has been found to be twice as reliable at predicting PTSD as the severity of the trauma itself. In other words: "[a soldier] could be mildly traumatized . . . and experience long-term PTSD simply because of a lack of social support back home" (p. 95).

Technology may not help. "Whatever the technological advances of modern society," says Junger, ". . . the individualized lifestyles that those technologies spawn seem to be deeply brutalizing to the human spirit" (p. 93).

Junger notes that "Israel is arguably the only modern country that retains a sufficient sense of community to mitigate the effects of combat on a mass scale" (p. 96). He quotes Dr. Arieh Shalev, who has studied PTSD for many years: "[Israelis] who come back from combat are reintegrated into a society where those experiences are very well understood." Shalev goes on to say that of "1,323 soldiers who were wounded in war and referred for psychiatric evaluation, only around 20% were diagnosed with PTSD and less than 2% retained that diagnosis three decades later" (p. 97). By contrast, writes Junger, PTSD is diagnosed in nearly 30% of the veterans treated by the U.S. Veterans Administration.

We, the denizens of the market, are not good to each other. Our loyalty is to an extremely narrow group of people: our children, our spouse, our parents, and a few close friends. The larger society is often alienating, technical, cold, and mystifying. It doesn't prioritize the human desire to be close to our fellows (www.thedailybeast.com/articles/2012/10/21/).

Psychological Distress and the Market System   17

Just in case Junger might seem too touchy-feely, here is what ex-General James "Mad-Dog" Mattis, the Secretary of Defense, had to say on the matter:

> Go back to Ben Franklin—his description of how the Iroquois Nations lived and worked together. Compare that to America today. I think that, when you look at veterans coming out of the wars, they're more and more just slapped in the face by that isolation, and they're used to something better. They think it's P.T.S.D.—which it can be—but it's really about alienation. If you lose any sense of being a part of something bigger, then why should you care about your fellow-man?
>
> (Filkins, 2017)

What Junger and Mattis have to say brilliantly highlights the relevance of social conditions to psychiatric conditions, not just to PTSD. Community can protect people even from horrendous circumstances; lack of it can breed distress. The market system doesn't do as much damage as war, but its de-emphasis of community can adversely affect people in similar ways.

* * *

The characteristics and features of the market system that we have identified contribute to various different types of psychological distress, but we are primarily concerned with only one kind—chronic, obsessive self-evaluation, the struggle to suppress the negative voice and reach high self-esteem. For many people this becomes a preoccupation that is central to their thinking and to their emotional life. As market-type thinking spreads into other areas of life, this preoccupation is likely to have an increasing effect on people's emotions. We'll look at how emotions function in the market system in the next chapter.

Notes

1. The term *lek* refers to an open area where male birds display to attract females.
2. There are many physical diseases of affluence—chronic, non-communicable diseases and other physical health conditions associated with prosperity. Examples include type 2 diabetes, asthma, coronary heart disease, cerebrovascular disease, peripheral vascular disease, obesity, hypertension, cancer, alcoholism, gout, and some types of allergy.

2 Ancient Emotions in a Strange New World

The Original Economy

Strange as it may seem, some of the unique characteristics of the human emotional system evolved, in large part, to regulate a socio-economic system. Not ours, of course, not the market system, but rather, the system of our hunter-gatherer ancestors. That system was based on reciprocity (reciprocal altruism)—a sense, a feeling of mutual obligation, a set of emotions. It was reciprocity and its emotions that regulated behavior; there were no police, no written laws, no courts.

And no money.[1] The "economy" of the group was based on sharing and the exchange of favors and gifts. When an animal was killed, everyone got some meat. If someone had an especially nice tool, it was soon given away. The few goods people did have circulated freely through the group. In economic terms, if you gave something, you created a debt; the recipients knew they "owed" you. If you received something, you owed in turn.

The system worked because everybody in one of those ancestral bands was related, by blood or marriage, and was dependent on the others. The reciprocity system wasn't a matter of goodness or generosity; it was a question of life and death. Favors, gifts, and sharing reinforced relationships and built trust. Cooperation demanded trust, and trust was essential for survival. Reciprocity for hunter-gatherers was both an "economic system" and a safety net.

The emotions humans have today were designed to work within those family groups, groups in which everyone shared feelings of mutual obligation and responsibility.

The Emotions

The emotions that helped to regulate this system were guilt, shame, gratitude, envy, greed, and what Robert Trivers (1971) calls "righteous indignation" (anger). This ensemble of emotions is unique to humans. It arose only

Ancient Emotions in a Strange New World 19

after we became hunter-gatherers, sometime after 250,000 years ago. Anger and fear are, of course, much older and some of the other emotions may have existed in incipient form in pre-human species, but our primate ancestors probably didn't experience much shame, guilt, or gratitude.

Guilt and shame, abetted by some fear, served to prevent our ancestors from doing things that could get them kicked out of the band—a sentence of death. Gratitude worked the same way; it induced them to respond in kind to the favors and gifts they received. Righteous anger, envy, and greed helped to ensure that individuals wouldn't allow themselves to be taken advantage of.

Together, these emotions create what we experience as a sense of *fairness* (Bronson and DeWaal, 2014). You knew what was coming to you and you knew what your obligations were. At least you thought you did. You had a sense . . .

Those nomads had no means of storing value and so they had no way to transmit wealth from one generation to the next—no crops, no amber waves of grain, no money. So no inheritance. And no taxes. They also couldn't afford to accumulate many possessions; carrying lots of stuff around would have been counterproductive. As a result, there was no way for an individual to "get ahead" by leaving the other members of the band behind.

This way of life had a number of consequences for the emotions. It meant that greed couldn't lead to wealth. It meant that inequality couldn't install itself and thereby generate rage. It meant that to a large extent, people could rely on their emotions to guide their behavior. The emotions were functional and indispensable.

There was nothing utopian about this system. Our nomadic ancestors were no better and no worse than we are, because they were, in fact, us. Or, rather, we are what they were. They complained, argued, had illicit trysts, fought, and killed each other, just as humans do today. But because they couldn't store wealth, each individual sought little more than survival, personal well-being, and the recognition of others.

The Rules of Reciprocity

Reciprocity operated according to certain rules. If one person gave another a knife or did someone a favor, the giver expected a gift or a favor in return. The payback didn't have to occur immediately; sometime in the future was good enough. Nor did the future gift have to be something of "equal value." Actually, it couldn't be. Since hunter-gatherers had no money, they had no way of measuring value precisely. But both giver and receiver (and their relatives) had a sense of what would be appropriate; people complained, loudly, to the whole band, if they thought they were being shorted.

20 *Ancient Emotions in a Strange New World*

Hunter-gatherer societies developed various mechanisms to prevent people from acquiring more than they needed. For example, among the !Kung of southern Africa, the hunter who shot an animal was *not* the person who decided how to divide up the meat. That privilege belonged to the owner of the fatal arrow. Since arrows were regularly given as gifts, the "owner" could be anyone, man or woman, young or old. This kind of rule prevented great hunters from getting more meat than other people. The only personal benefit such a hunter got was the respect of others.

In the reciprocity system, family and economy were one and the same thing, so the emotions could regulate *all* behavior effectively. That, obviously, is not the case today. Family and workplace operate according to very different principles. As a result, the emotions aren't particularly well-suited to life in organizations (see Chapter 4). Much of the distress that people experience today is the result of this mismatch.

The Persistence of the Emotions

Nevertheless, as readers will already have noted, the emotions underlying the reciprocity system are still with us today. We feel gratitude toward those who give to us and guilt if we don't reciprocate. We keep track of who owes whom what. We resent those who are selfish or greedy. We feel slighted if someone doesn't reciprocate. We feel guilt and shame if we shirk our own responsibilities or cheat our friends. We expect our friends and relatives to behave in similar fashion. If they don't, we get disappointed and angry. In other words, we continue to base our personal lives and behavior on these emotions.

The problem is that many people bring these expectations to their interactions with the rest of the world—strangers, casual acquaintances, and institutions. And there, quite literally, is the rub.

The Real World

Obviously, the emotions don't regulate the world we live in today. To begin with, few people now live in a "universe of kin." Instead, they live in big groups full of strangers with whom they often have only the most minimal connection. We humans want to trust people, but it is difficult to know where we can and when it's safe to relax. The price for some people is constant vigilance.

Our economic system does not operate according to the rules of reciprocity. Our society is based on money and money *ends* relationships; it doesn't form and reinforce them. Once you've paid for something, you're quits. You can just walk away. Paying people money for their labor or time relieves

Ancient Emotions in a Strange New World 21

an employer of further obligation (unless the law intervenes). Supervisors believe they're entitled to say, "I pay you a good wage for a good day's work. What are you complaining about?"

We do complain, because we expect something more human. Often without knowing why, we expect reciprocity—we expect to be valued, we expect recognition, we expect "fairness."

Fairness for a human being isn't about measuring "equal amounts" of money or things. It's about recognition of one's contribution and about the level of respect implied in the reward. Someone who mutters about lack of fairness when a new employee is hired at a higher salary is feeling disrespected.

Unfairness breeds comparison and self-evaluation. In the market system, it's a small step, psychologically, from "that's unfair" to "what's wrong with me?"

Fairness and reciprocity are part of a human being's biological equipment, but money isn't. That's why money isn't enough. It isn't what makes us feel good. Just listen to millionaire ballplayers complaining about being treated unfairly. They talk about respect.

Two studies done by Daniel Kahneman and Angus Deaton (2010) showed that emotional well-being is related to money only to the point that people have "enough" (about $75,000 at that time). After that, other things, such as being with family and friends, or collaborating with others on a successful project, become more important. Kahneman and Deaton also discovered that there is quite a gap between "emotional well-being" (what actually makes people happy) and "life evaluation" (what people *think* will make them happy). The participants in the study thought that more money would make them happier, even though it didn't.

The ancient reciprocity system continues to play a significant role in our ideological and political life. The emotions make us uncomfortable with, and conflicted about, economic inequality. On one level, inequality breeds envy and greed: envy if we have less than others or less than we think we should have, greed if there is a possibility of adding to our possessions and status. But just to make things more complicated, many of us feel guilt and shame when we see that *we* have more than others. It hurts our sense of fairness. That's almost certainly why many well-off people vote for candidates and parties that speak in the name of the underprivileged and the poor. The emotions have their say no matter where we sit on the totem pole.

Above all, the gap between what one has and what others have fosters comparison. Comparison in turn leads to self-evaluation: "Am I as good as . . ." (fill in the blanks):

- The guy next door?
- My colleague who got the promotion?

22 *Ancient Emotions in a Strange New World*

- My boss wants me to be?
- I should be?

All these versions of "am I good enough?" are corrosive.

Equal opportunity, the central ideology of the American market system, fosters further self-evaluation and ultimately self-doubt. Equal opportunity means that if you're smart and work hard, you'll be successful. So, people conclude: "If I'm not successful I'm either not smart enough or I'm not working hard enough." All this questioning can lead to a kind of permanent preoccupation with the self and a desperate struggle for self-esteem.

The Emotions in the Organization

Humans have, of course, brought their emotions to modern organizations. For example, people can feel, for their city, their country, their church, their corporation, or their football team, the same fierce loyalty that our ancestors once felt for the band.

Organizations exploit these emotions. They make endless demands on us and trick us into meeting those demands by masquerading as the family. They do whatever they can to get us to work as hard as we did when our survival depended on it.

Part of this exploitation just happens, but part of it is designed. Organizations create teams. Whether the managers know it or not, the teams mimic the band. We respond. We stay late. We meet arbitrary deadlines. We stay glued to our communication devices, lest a demand go unanswered. We cut back on our time with spouses and children. We *feel* a part of something, and that feels good. For the moment.

But the organization is not the band. The members of a team are only provisionally interdependent. Any individual can be laid off; it's not ostracism but it can feel like it.

The wise man and woman must, unfortunately, beware of the feelings that guided human behavior in the ancient days. This unnatural wariness builds still another conflict into the psyche.

There is, of course, an element of rationality in our loyalty to organizations. Our fates are in fact linked, for a time, with the organizations we work for and in. Our chances of doing well are greater if our organization does well.

Furthermore, it is true that these same emotions make it *possible* for humans to create massive organizations and to work effectively in them, an ability that has allowed us to conquer the planet. But that is small consolation to the individuals who find themselves at sea in the sea of humanity.

Self-Promotion and the Emotions

The market system rewards self-promotion. People today can be famous for being famous. Executives are encouraged to be aggressive. Students in business school are taught to establish their personal *brand*. Those who can do this comfortably are often highly successful. They make a lot of money and acquire great status.

Our ancestors, on the other hand, evolved in societies that frowned on boasting. That's probably why some contemporaries are reluctant to stand out. The message—promote thyself in order to succeed—causes many people to experience anxiety. They don't feel comfortable singing their own praises. The pressure to do so often pushes them to measure themselves against others, and that, as we have pointed out, leads to self-evaluation, self-criticism, and the struggle for high self-esteem.

Opportunity and Identity

So many options, so little time. The endless opportunities are one of the glories of the market system but not everybody enjoys them. For some, having so many options is confusing. It means that they have to invent their identity instead of growing into it naturally, as humans were designed to do. Some people thrive on creating and recreating themselves; some do not. For those who do not, identity becomes fused with self-evaluation. Who am I? Am I good enough? Compared to what? Or whom? This disruption of identity can be wounding. People are spending their lives trying to figure out whether they are OK or not. To a large extent, they come to therapy to get help with this task.

* * *

In the next chapter we'll look at some of the strange characteristics of modern childhood.

Note

1. Some bands traded with others using shells as a kind of proto-currency.

3 Children of the Market System

Trauma, neglect, abandonment. No one need be reminded of the existence of child abuse. It's in the papers on an all-too-regular basis. It seems to plague all existing social systems. The market system is no exception, but it may not be any worse than all the other systems.

On the other hand, various features of the market system expose children to damage of a more subtle kind. These features hide in plain sight. We take them for granted. In fact, we don't think of them as problems.

The features we are referring to include parenting behind walls, the nuclear family, the age cohort, discipline, competition, and comparison. We'll look at them one by one, but they are actually all connected. They have one thing in common. They all tend to promote self-evaluation, which, when these children grow up, can turn chronic and obsessive.

Parenting Behind Walls

When children are raised behind closed doors, what goes on between parent and child is shielded from the eyes of the community. In the privacy of the home, systematic deviation from community norms becomes possible. Privacy opens the way for hypocrisy. Children can be "entrusted" with secrets, information that they are told to keep from strangers. This can promote shame around natural functions such as sex, reproduction, and excretion. Freud's terror of the primal scene in the marital bed was a product of Viennese culture, not a natural phenomenon.

When we look back at our hunting-gathering ancestors, what jumps out is that they had no walls. With the exception of initiation ceremonies, adulterous trysts, and the like, virtually every aspect of life was visible to the children. Shame over natural functions was almost certainly impossible.

This open-plan living also meant that the parents could not easily abuse children. They would have had to do it in front of all their peers, including

Children of the Market System   25

the children's aunts, uncles, and cousins. Those relatives weren't likely to tolerate major deviations from the norm.

Besides, for nomadic peoples, children were the "wealth" of the band and the only possible safety net. The adults had no savings and there were no government programs to support them in old age. As a result, the older folk had a strong incentive to cherish the offspring. Here's a typical ethnographic observation from an anthropologist who studied the Mardudjara aborigines of western Australia:

> Within a few days of birth, the infant becomes the center of attention in the camp surrounded almost continuously by siblings and older relatives who shower it with affection. Adults show extreme indulgence toward children of all ages, and a crying child can be sure of a quick response from its mother and others nearby, who pacify it by acceding to its demands.
>
> (Tonkinson, 1978, p. 64)

Walls make abuse possible. They also make it possible for parents to implement idiosyncratic approaches to parenting that fall short of abuse. Excessive pressure to succeed or to conform, favoritism, indifference, and a host of other potentially damaging parenting practices become possible when parenting is shielded from view.

The Nuclear Family

We take the nuclear family for granted, but it's not a natural phenomenon. Throughout our history as a species, children grew up in larger groups— bands and extended families. A nuclear family can provide certain advantages, but there are problems.

Within a nuclear family, the two parents loom awfully large. They can acquire a great deal of power. They can dominate the lives of their children even when they don't intend to. Some children can handle this kind of regime well; others can't. The proliferation of *how-to-parent* books testifies to the difficulty people have finding the right parenting strategies.

In the historically most common version of the nuclear family, the father is absent from the home during the day. The workplace is out of view. Children can observe only a limited range of adult activities, so they can't learn what they will need to know about adult life solely by observation and imitation. And because the labor of the father is not observable by the children, his contribution to their welfare can go unappreciated, even though he may be working desperately hard. His children may be experiencing him as a tired, distant giant who ignores them or is expected to discipline them: "Just wait 'til your father gets home."

26 *Children of the Market System*

Currently, this situation may apply equally to the mother. And where the mother is still a homemaker who doesn't work outside the home, she is often left to do her duties without the company of other adults. Many women in this situation end up bored, irritable, and depressed.

When both parents are working out of the home, the situation can be even worse. While good professional care can be a viable substitute for parental involvement, it isn't always, and many people cannot afford good professional care. Without any outward appearance of neglect, children can grow up feeling unloved and unsure of their value.

Among our hunter-gatherer ancestors, no parent was left all day with only children for company. No adults were stuck in a room and driven out of their minds with a screaming child or two. Every adult was involved in keeping all the children safe and connected. Consequently, as anthropologist Colin Turnbull says about the Mbuti (Pygmies) of the Ituri rainforest, "it is no accident that [an Mbuti] child calls everyone in the same age group as his parents 'father' or 'mother'; those still older are called 'grandparent'" (Turnbull, 1961, p. 126). Being embedded in an extended family, all of whom participate in your upbringing, might seem suffocating to many today, but it gave hunter-gatherer children a deep sense of both safety and connection with others. A child was already one of the people, related to everyone, of value to the whole group. It was a very different environment for children—and for their parents.

The Age Cohort

Children in our current society spend a great deal of their time—in school, in church, in sports, etc.—in age cohorts and are expected to perform in a manner "appropriate to their age." But in reality children develop according to different schedules; some grow up much more quickly than others. The tyranny of the age cohort singles out both the high and low achievers for differential treatment. The "stars" often get "gifted and talented" enrichment programs in school; if they don't, they end up bored and alienated. The "laggards" often get special education resource rooms; if they don't, they end up lost. Children who might eventually mature into fully functional adults can spend years being perceived as impaired or deficient, simply because they are being measured by an inappropriate standard.

Among our hunter-gatherer ancestors, children grew up in mixed age groups. Older children watched out for the younger ones. All the children developed at their own speed. Children only undertook adult tasks when they were ready, not according to a standard timetable. The Utku (Eskimo), says Jean Briggs,

> don't believe there is any point in trying to teach a child before he is ready; the child is permitted to time his own social growth. The belief is

Children of the Market System 27

that the more *ihuma* (maturity; good sense) the child acquires, the more he will want to use it. Adults just wait for him to conform.

(Briggs, 1970, pp. 111–112)

Discipline

"Discipline" is such an essential feature of parenting in today's system that we take the need for it as natural. And today there is a need. The world has become exceedingly complicated. Children must somehow be prepared for the different challenges they might end up facing. Since they can't learn enough through observation and imitation, they can't be left on their own to discover the world by themselves. Adults now have to provide *instruction*, and that requires discipline.

Hunter-gatherer children were rarely disciplined. The only time adults corrected or punished children was when they hurt other children or behaved in anti-social ways. Among the Mardudjara, for example, temper tantrums

> are tolerated with great patience and resignation by adults. . . . The offended child is rarely disciplined unless it is jealously threatening violence against a younger sibling or one of its parents at a time when they feel unwell.
>
> (Tonkinson, 1978, pp. 64–65)

Hunter-gatherer parents could afford to be permissive. They didn't have to worry about how children would turn out because willy-nilly the children were going to become adult hunter-gatherers and members of the band; there was no alternative lifestyle. Consequently children could be allowed to develop at their own pace. The !Kung say that children who throw tantrums or behave badly have not yet acquired their "intelligence." There is no doubt in a !Kung parent's mind that as children grow up they will

> learn to act with sense, with or without deliberate training, simply as a result of maturation, social pressure and the desire to conform to group values. Since most Kung adults are cooperative, generous, and hard-working, and seem to be no more self-centered than any other people, this theory is evidently right, at least for them.
>
> (Shostak, 1981, p. 149)

Competition

Kids who live in a market system are thrown into competition with one another early in life. In school, pupils have to vie for grades. Teachers often grade "on the curve," which means that there can only be so many As and an

28 *Children of the Market System*

equal number of Fs. Understandably, teachers employ competitive games, such as spelling bees and math contests. Kids who want to play sports have to try out for a spot on the team. Kids who want to play music have to audition for a place in the orchestra. Eventually, kids compete to get into good colleges.

Recently, social media has become a competition. Kids compete with other kids for having the most friends, for texting the most outrageous messages, for posting the coolest selfies. In inner cities, gangs compete over turf and respect. The entire world of childhood and adolescence is a competitive arena.

This state of affairs, however problematic, makes perfect sense. When adults have to compete for jobs, promotions, raises, and recognition, a culture of competition will come to dominate childhood as well. Adults who have to compete not surprisingly believe that children must be introduced to competition when they're young so that they will be able to compete when they grow up. Parents understandably push their kids to do better, try harder, get better grades, and, above all, win. Nobody wants a loser.

Who knows what shadows fall on the souls of children who are raised to compete with those who are close. That kind of competition builds a contradiction into the mind. Some survive unscathed. Some don't.

Comparison

Comparison is the handmaiden of competition. To compete effectively, one has to judge one's performance against the efforts and accomplishments of others. It's almost impossible to avoid watching and weighing what others do.

Like competition, comparison begins at an early age, and is often fueled by parents. Many parents compare their kids' achievements to those of siblings and other children: "Your brother does his chores, why can't you do yours?" "If you lost some weight, you'd be prettier than . . ." "If you studied harder, you'd get good grades like . . ." "If you practiced more, you'd play piano better than . . ." "Why didn't you try out for football? You're a better athlete than . . ."

When parents send the message that nothing but "the best" is good enough, high levels of stress are inevitable, and the kids who aren't among the best often can't help developing negative opinions of themselves: "I'll never be able to please my parents." "I'll never be popular because I'm not pretty." And finally, the ultimate conclusion: "I'm not good enough."

Even hidden, this message can leak out. Children can, of course, sense the disappointment of parents (or other adults, including relatives and teachers). Some interpret it as a judgment. Some turn it into self-judgment.

Aldo is a case in point. He had a new job and was doing well:

Th: Did your success help you to dismiss your thoughts about not being good enough?

Cl: To some extent, not completely.

Th: So what makes those thoughts so compelling?

Cl: I think it's because of my mother's standards. She always pushed me to do better. She didn't put me down, but I got the message.

Th: Can you give me an example?

Cl: She pushed me to apply to a top Boston college. I didn't want to go there, but she implied that if I didn't apply, it would mean I wasn't good enough.

Th: What about your father?

Cl: He was much less educated. He was more laissez faire and easygoing. Mother had the upper hand, made the decisions. She was often dissatisfied with him.

Th: Did you identify with your father?

Cl: Yes, very much so.

Since hunter-gatherer children weren't set up to compete with each other, occasions to compare were far less frequent. No grades, no races, no organized sports. All the children could see what their adult role both should and would be. Furthermore, since there was no means of storing value and therefore no wealth, children lived in a world of basic equality. There was no mountain of socio-economic success to climb or to foster envy.

Identity and Self-Evaluation

The children of the market system have the same need to participate, affiliate, and belong as the children of their foraging ancestors had. But what a different world they live in! And what a daunting task—to manufacture an identity for themselves! They can't simply morph automatically into adult members of a community. From an early age, the pressure is on to *become* something or other, and parents often have idiosyncratic ideas about what that something ought to be. Even children whose parents encourage them to explore their talents and interests can be paralyzed by the bewildering number of available options. As we have pointed out before, a common result of this upbringing is a tendency to confuse obsessive, chronic self-evaluation with exploration and discovery.

***

In the next chapter, we will look more closely at the problems of work in the market system.

4 Work

Oppression or Opportunity?

"I was tired, depressed, and no longer enjoying a job I had once loved. To stay in my position I had been paying an increasingly heavy price in pressure, politics, and stress. I was losing perspective." So writes Elizabeth Perle McKenna on page one of *When Work Doesn't Work Any More* (1997). McKenna's book is focused on the problems of women in the workforce, but clearly many men suffer similarly from stress, frustration, anger, and confusion. As we noted in Chapter 1, organizations grounded in competition and hierarchy can create problems for anyone.

Some people seem to thrive in these institutions, but many don't. Those who don't wonder why they don't get promotions, why the boss doesn't pay more attention to them, why colleagues don't like them, why subordinates don't have more respect for them. Even those who do thrive often become disenchanted with their jobs and begin to wonder who they really are. McKenna herself was a successful professional in a publishing house before she quit.

When we look at the original human form of organization—the social organization that molded our genetic predispositions—the reason is obvious: Human beings weren't designed to live in large, impersonal organizations. One might even say they weren't designed to work. In this chapter we'll take a closer look at the relationship between the problems that people bring to therapists and the institutions of the market system.

The Vicissitudes of Size

As noted in previous chapters, our hunter-gatherer ancestors lived among relatives in small bands; everyone knew everyone else intimately. Band members had to do pretty much everything together—raise children, forage for food, make tools, dance, tell stories, perform healing ceremonies—so they witnessed many sides of all their band mates. In the process, they learned, among other things, who could be trusted and who, if anyone, could not.

Work 31

People today may work among thousands of strangers and yet have nothing to do with any of them outside the workplace. The private lives of co-workers usually remain out of sight. The ambiance of the elevator could perhaps serve as a metaphor: strangers standing around staring at the ground, saying nothing. Under these conditions, it's very difficult, if not impossible, to know who is trustworthy, and it is very easy to feel disconnected, untethered, and unsure.

The Uncertainty of Identity

As noted in previous chapters, identity, in a band, was based on belonging; people grew up knowing who they were. Today, that isn't guaranteed. To establish a stable identity is not so easy. Even "belonging" is often not clear. Families break apart. Friends and relatives move away. Children go from school to school. In the cities and the towns, diversity rules. Eventually, children who are struggling to figure out who they are have to enter the market system where identity is based on achievement.

Here's how McKenna first viewed the marketplace:

> I assumed that having money paved the path to a happy life and would open a world of independence and freedom at my feet. A "good job" meant travel, a vice presidency, and having enough money that I'd never have to depend on a husband even if he could afford to provide for me. Success would be marked by having a corner office thirty-two floors above Sixth Avenue and Fiftieth Street Manhattan with a rust-colored suede couch and matching chair.
>
> (McKenna, 1997, p. 43)

But as time went on, she became disenchanted with both her identity and her success, as the quote at the beginning of this chapter testifies.

When people with unclear or fractured identities enter the workplace, they can come to imagine that they are *members* of the organization—not just employees. The organization slides into the spot that was designed, by evolution, for the band. But unlike the band, the organization can let you go. So when things go wrong, or even when a boss doesn't seem appreciative enough, people whose sense of self is wrapped up in the job can easily spin into negative self-evaluations: "Was it my fault?" "Am I doing something wrong?" Losing one's job becomes a catastrophe some people never recover from.

The Relativity of Status

In a band, status was unambiguous. Status came from the appreciation and respect of the others in the group. If you were good at something—or if you

32   *Work*

were strong, fast, observant—your skill and knowledge helped the others and they responded. Everyone knew what you contributed and recognized it. You knew it too.

In modern organizations, status is a bit more problematic. First of all, not everyone feels they have status; some people, as the saying goes, just get no respect. Second, status doesn't necessarily depend on doing things for the group. Just making money or acquiring power can provide status. One can even get status by showing off, sporting expensive cars, or wearing fashionable clothes.

It is possible, of course, to acquire status by doing things for the organization, but even then there's a problem. People now belong to many groups; what benefits one group can actually create conflict with another. For example, doing what's best for one's employer might mean laying off team members, uprooting the family, or polluting the environment. The very thing that provides status in some people's eyes may generate resentment in the minds of others.

Thus, the natural desire for status can put people in unnatural positions, leading some individuals to ruminate endlessly on their roles and identities.

The Inevitability of Comparison

The child who grows up comparing will have to continue comparing as an adult. It is virtually impossible to work in a hierarchical organization without comparing oneself to others. The structure of the organization forces people to match their self-evaluation with the evaluations of their colleagues and hierarchical superiors, a procedure that is institutionalized in the excruciating ritual of the "annual review."

Comparison can be deadly. The decisions about staffing and promotion that are made in large organizations often have little to do with ability. Seniority, nepotism, and an insecure leader's need to hire people he or she can control often trump competence. In a study of organizational behavior, Fred Luthans and his team discovered that "successful" managers—those who got promoted—spent more of their time cultivating their superiors than working with colleagues or subordinates. As one successful manager put it,

> I find that the way to get ahead around here is to be friendly with the right people, both inside and outside the firm. They get tired of always talking shop, so I find a common interest—with some it's sports, with others it's our kids—and interact with them on that level. The other formal stuff around the office is important, but I really work at this informal side and have found it pays off when promotion time rolls around.
>
> (Luthans, 1988, p. 132)

In the meantime, other managers might be making themselves sick wondering why someone else got the promotion, when that someone was just better at kissing up.

Now there's even a movie about comparison. *Brad's Status* is all about Brad's obsessive concern with his relative position in the world. Brad is successful, but his friends are doing better and his son seems likely to outdo him. No one seems to think Brad's concern is odd. Indeed, film critic Christy Lemire describes it as "the human tendency to take stock, especially around middle age, and to compare our lives against both our friends' achievements and our youthful visions of our future selves" (Lemire, 2017).

In an interview with *Fresh Air* host Terry Gross, the director Mike White said that "his latest film was born of his own status anxiety—an anxiety that sometimes keeps him up at night." White describes the compulsion to compare and how that compulsion is exacerbated by social media:

> It's a universal situation, but I also think that now more than ever with social media and the way you can access people's lives through Googling each other or getting on Instagram, you're just kind of more aware of, like, the curated lives of your contemporaries. And I think that creates a sense of anxiety or a sense of lack and feeling like "Is somebody's vacation better than mine?" or "Is someone having a better life than mine?"
>
> (*Fresh Air*, September 7, 2017)

Clearly, relative failure has become a feature of American life.

Competition Among Co-Workers

One of the more damaging aspects of competition within the system is confusion. "Do I compete or do I cooperate?" "Are we on the same team or are we working against each other?" Members of the teams fostered by enlightened organizations are often pitted against each other for promotion. When one company merges with or is taken over by another, employees have to fight it out for the remaining jobs. Promotions are often cast as overt competitions. This kind of environment can be devastating for losers, but even winners often get stressed out. Like children who are forced into competition with those who are close to them, employees who must compete with people they are supposed to cooperate with can be confused and doubly stressed.

Leadership and Authority

As far as one can tell, the organizations of our ancestors were flat. There were no permanent positions of authority, no hereditary chiefs, no bosses.

34 Work

People did, in certain circumstances, choose to follow an individual who had demonstrated superior ability, but this was purely voluntary. To be someone whose opinion carried weight in a band one had to be competent, experienced, and knowledgeable.

A good hunter had authority in the hunt because he had a record of success. But this authority did not automatically extend to any other area of life. Even shamans were only special during the ceremonies they performed; the rest of the time they were just people. This is why members of so-called "primitive tribes" often stared uncomprehendingly when Western explorers asked "Who is your leader?"

Influence and leadership were functions of merit. Here's an example. Among the Netsilik Inuit (Eskimo) recognized leaders were called "*inhumataqs*," a term which was translated by Western anthropologists as "headman." But it really means "the one who thinks" (Balikci, 1970, p. 116) and his job was to think about the welfare of the whole band.

The *inhumataq's* only reward was the respect he got if he did his job well. His position brought no special power or privilege. The others did not obey him, nor was he exempt from any tasks. He held his position only if he was effective. If an *inhumataq* wasn't competent, someone else would assume the responsibility. An incompetent *inhumataq* wouldn't actually be deposed; there would be no official action. People would simply begin to pay more attention to someone else.

Leadership scholars would call *inhumataqs* "emergent" leaders (Northouse, 2016). Emergent leaders are people who become leaders through competence, knowledge, charisma, and/or trustworthiness, not because they have official positions.

Northouse calls the people who occupy official positions *assigned* leaders. Their position in the hierarchy, and not their personal characteristics, gives them the authority to control the behavior of others.

There are, of course, emergent leaders in hierarchical organizations, and they can play important roles, but their leadership is usually indirect and often goes unacknowledged. There were no assigned leaders in the band.

Being an assigned leader comes with problems. People tend to resent them and they often suffer from the resentment they engender. Furthermore, they are often held responsible for organizational outcomes that they have no control over. Here's how McKenna describes the situation of a manager whose organization was becoming more hierarchical:

> Jane began to feel undervalued and underappreciated. Because of the increasing layers of hierarchy, she found she had increasing amounts of responsibility and decreasing amounts of authority. Someone was added to her staff without her having been so much as consulted, and

Work 35

she, in turn, had to fire the employee after a year of time-consuming training proved fruitless.

(McKenna, 1997, p. 34)

The Need to Cooperate

Competition is, of course, the life blood of the market system. But our species came into being because our ancestors learned how to cooperate. The need to feel like a participant in a cooperative endeavor is still strong and finds expression in various ways. For example, the Luthans team that identified "successful" managers also identified what they called "effective" managers. These were managers who focused on teambuilding and getting a job done. The "effective" managers spent time creating relationships with their colleagues and subordinates. Said one:

> Both how much and how well things get done around here, as well as keeping my people loyal and happy, has to do with keeping them informed and involved. If I make a change in procedure or the guys upstairs give us a new process or piece of equipment to work with, I get my people's input and give them the full story before I lay it on them. Then I make sure they have the proper training and give them feedback on how they are doing. When they screw up, I let them know it, but when they do a good job, I let them know about that too.
>
> (Luthans, 1988, p. 133)

Unfortunately, according to Luthans, *effective* managers don't get promoted as often as managers who cultivate their superiors to seek personal advancement. The desire to be cooperative is often thwarted by the system.

Falling Behind

Being an assigned leader may be no picnic, but failing to rise in the hierarchy generally feels even worse. Getting passed over consistently for promotion and/or not getting jobs for which you think you are qualified is painful. Russ was such an individual. He was the quintessential bottom dog. He couldn't figure out how to operate in a hierarchical world. The problems he faced and the responses he was getting from the world forced him into negative self-evaluation.

Russ was a new assistant facilities manager at a high-tech company. He did not have a strong work history. He had actually been fired from his previous job because of his all-to-human demands. He had been doing the job he was hired to do very well, but he kept requesting that he be given more

36 *Work*

responsibilities and more authority. In the opinion of his employer, this was unreasonable. He had come to therapy because he didn't want to repeat the experience, but he was starting to run into trouble again:

Cl: I really like the job and the company. I've been thinking about letting people know that I could do a lot more.

Th: Have you been asked to?

Cl: Not really.

Th: Who's doing those things now?

Cl: My boss. But he has less experience than me.

Th: What's he like?

Cl: He's a nervous guy, always running around. Pretty busy.

Th: Sounds like he might be easily threatened. I think you should wait until you're asked to do things. Your job is to make your boss look good. If you show him up, you will make an enemy, and you are likely to lose.

Cl: OK. But there's something else that bothers me.

Th: What's that?

Cl: I'm not sure people like me there. Some of the people don't even answer when I say hi.

Th: Are these mostly the technical staff?

Cl: Yeah, mostly. I feel like I'm doing something wrong.

Th: OK, listen. You are in a hierarchical organization. Humans aren't designed to live in them. We're designed to live in relatively egalitarian communities. The way those people are treating you has nothing to do with you personally. It's the way people in hierarchical organizations treat people below them. That's why many people don't like hierarchical organizations. But we're stuck with them.

After considerable discussion, Russ proposed a solution:

Cl: Well, would it help to tell them that I'm a musician in a band that plays a lot locally? That would raise my status, wouldn't it?

Th: I doubt it. If you make a friend there, you can tell him, but to announce it as a way of improving your status might make things worse.

Cl: Why?

Th: They might see you as boasting. They might not want to know that you are a musician because then they would have a conflict.

Cl: What kind of conflict?

Th: Your status would be unclear. They wouldn't know how to treat you and that would make them uncomfortable. Which isn't in your best interests.

Work 37

Cl: Some people might think you're pretty cynical.

Th: Maybe so, but when you have a position in an organization, you have to play the role that goes with that position. You send the *role* to work, not your real self. Don't put yourself on the line to be judged.

Cl: Even with my team?

Th: Your team is not a team. Wait, let me correct that. Your team is not your band. It's a pseudo team. It's only a team for work purposes, not something you belong to for real.

Cl: So I should try to be accepted?

Th: Listen, acceptance isn't a breeze that wafts across your cheeks just like the winds caress the trees. It's in your head. *You* have to accept you and you have to take pride in your role, as long as you're in it.

Russ was relieved. He vowed to abandon the self-defeating strategies that lost him his previous job. More importantly, he felt he was able to stop agonizing about his deficiencies.

Getting Ahead

Hierarchical organizations are essential components of the market system. They offer enormous opportunities for wealth and status, but there are costs. The stress of competition, the unavoidable comparisons with others, and the constant uncertainty of one's position—all can be debilitating. Like it or not, life in such organizations is the new normal. But, as we have seen, the new normal is not so normal for human beings, and the gap between what is normal now and what was normal as we evolved is rather large.

Val was at the opposite end of the spectrum from Russ. He was making a lot of money as a salesman in a major company and was frequently named salesman of the month. That meant free trips to romantic islands and other coveted prizes. But the pressure was extreme:

Cl: You can't imagine what it's like. The pressure is crazy. There's no let-up. Once you hit a goal, they up it. If you don't reach the new goal, they start humiliating you. They post your results. My boss singles me out—when I do good and when I don't. You can never rest on your laurels. They insinuate that you're not trying. Or that you're over the hill. So you start beating yourself up. Then you work like crazy to prove to yourself that you're not the useless bastard they are making you out to be.

Most people don't experience this kind of overt, systematic humiliation and this extreme carrot and stick regime, but it doesn't take all that much to trigger punishing self-evaluation in the average human being.

38   *Work*

Top dog, bottom dog. Hierarchy hurts if you have hunter-gatherer ancestors.

Oppression or Opportunity?

How do you view your job? A lot depends on how you view yourself. When Karl came in, he was writhing in a sea of self-criticism. He had an urgent need to prove to himself that he was a super-performer. For years, he had stretched himself to meet the endless needs of his company and condemned himself for failing. But now he had turned hostile. He was blaming the company and his bosses for his anxiety and depression. He was seeing himself as a victim.

We did a tour of his jobs. He had worked while in high school, mostly because he wanted things that his family couldn't or wouldn't provide. He worked throughout his college years, again to get stuff. Each job he got seemed like an opportunity. But once he graduated, he began to resent the jobs he got. He began to feel that his willingness to work hard was being exploited. Slowly, jobs morphed from opportunity to oppression.

We were eventually able to find the origins of this transformation. He recalled that when he was growing up, his mother had had a job that she hated, something on a night shift. She would make a big deal of her dissatisfaction. Worse, his parents had to wake him up when mother went to work, at 10 p.m. or so, to take him with them to her job, because they couldn't leave him alone. He had ended up with her negative approach to work.

In therapy, Karl finally realized that he didn't have to be a perfect servant of the organization. He began to accept his imperfections, and as he did so, his attitude toward the job began to change back to what it had been. Once again, he saw the opportunities that were there and could plan to take advantage of them. He attributed his breakthrough to a phrase that came up in a previous session, the phrase that serves as the heading for this segment: oppression or opportunity?

* * *

All the factors we have identified in this chapter can foster self-evaluation. Any one of them, at any given time, can push it up toward the grandiose or push it down toward the abject. In the next chapter we will begin to lay out a treatment strategy designed specifically to counteract this wasteful, often self-defeating process.

5 Imaginary Sticks, Imaginary Stones

Undoing Self-Generated Distress

Let's review. Many jobs in our market system make endless demands, provide little praise, emphasize the aggressive and competitive emotions, force people to choose between work and family, push people to compare themselves with others, and rely on cold cash to motivate rather than on biologically meaningful rewards. As a result, people often end up struggling with a strongly negative self-evaluation—even if they are doing fine, materially. This struggle, when it exists, is a particularly productive avenue for therapy.

The Struggle

In order to exit from the struggle, clients need to stop evaluating themselves, either positively or negatively. Simply put, self-evaluation is a major contributor to psychological distress. Not just *negative* self-evaluation. Any self-evaluation. The procedure itself is corrupt, whether its findings are positive or negative. There should be no trials in the courtroom of the self.

With hindsight, one can see that Albert Ellis, one of the two great founders of cognitive therapy, had this realization many years ago. But Ellis used a different technique to undermine self-evaluation. He ridiculed it, called it "must-erbation," and got people to sing songs making fun of it.

I don't have the nerve or the desire to emulate his technique, but he was right. The people who come for psychotherapy are often, if not always, struggling to think highly of themselves because they are menaced by low self-esteem. They keep reaching for high self-esteem because they crave it. As a result, they often oscillate back and forth, endlessly, without being able to pin their self-evaluation in the positive position.

You can't win an argument with yourself. There is no win there and no winner.

Rating the self doesn't work. To stop doing it, people have to realize that they are engaged in a Sisyphean task. They might go up, but they will come

40 *Imaginary Sticks, Imaginary Stones*

down. To come out ahead, they will have to find another way to feel good. They will have to accept themselves as they are.

To avoid misunderstanding, it's necessary to distinguish between self-evaluation and identity. Self-evaluation involves comparison and a rating: *I'm better than . . . I'm worse than . . . I'm ahead of . . . I'm behind . . .* Identity, on the other hand, can and should be independent of both rating and comparison. A robust identity is based on belonging: *I'm a member of a family . . . I'm an American . . .* It can include all kinds of personal characteristics: *I like . . . I want . . . I think . . . I believe . . . I feel . . . I help . . . I participate . . .*

The same can be said for "self-image." Self-evaluation is one kind of self-image, the kind that involves a rating. It is possible to have a self-image that is not a rating, but a rating-free self-image is often difficult for us denizens of the market system to conjure up.

Unfortunately, there is an enormous amount of pressure in the market system to conflate identity and self-image with a rating.

The flat-out rejection of self-evaluation is perhaps the most controversial aspect of the approach outlined in this book. As noted in the Introduction, the rejection of self-evaluation brings us into potential conflict with one of the most cherished ideas in psychotherapy, the idea that the unexamined life is not worth living. Examining a life is, of course, what we do in therapy, but the purpose should be to free the client from the kind of perpetual self-examination that can be satisfied only by a rating.

Why High Self-Esteem Is Not the Solution

There are a number of reasons. As stated before, high self-esteem is hard to maintain in a steady state. It can be easily undone by setbacks, and it can easily merge into grandiosity. Recent research has brought another problem to light. Lynn O'Connor et al. (2001) have done studies showing that people who view themselves as more successful, or more able, or more privileged than others—people who compare themselves favorably with others—often feel guilty about their good fortune. O'Connor calls this a form of survival guilt.

There is some evolutionary sense to this. Anthropological accounts indicate that being better off than your fellows could be a precarious situation in ancestral social environments. For example, in *The Forest People* anthropologist Colin Turnbull tells of a kind of hunting magic that some members of an Mbuti band practiced. These families were

> highly criticized by the others as being antisocial. They were trying to get success for themselves at the expense of the others. On one such

Imaginary Sticks, Imaginary Stones 41

occasion a family had a long run of good luck, the animals always falling into their net, while others had no luck at all. It was decided that this must have been due to *anjo,* as the medicine was called, so everyone, including the offenders, agreed that the only thing to do was to destroy the horns that held the medicine.

(Turnbull, 1961, p. 96)

O'Connor proposes that this form of "survivor" guilt has been selected by evolution as a psychological mechanism facilitating group living. Be that as it may, the mechanism helps to explain the fact that materially successful individuals are often miserable. It also helps to explain why, as we noted in Chapter 2, large numbers of materially successful Americans often vote for candidates who promise to do something about poverty and inequality.

Survival guilt of this kind—let's call it "market-made guilt"—can, for example, contribute to depression. People who are depressed, says O'Connor, often have a distorted interpretation of what causes the pain of others; they blame themselves (O'Connor et al., 2001). If they're comparing, they're likely to see a lot of pain. The upshot: Comparison is a losing game, whether you think you're the greatest or the worst.

Obviously, not everyone gets depressed because of market-made guilt, but its existence helps to ensure that people operating in the system will have confusing and contradictory feelings. Again, some people can cope very well with these conditions; others struggle.

In sum: Negative self-evaluation is bad but positive self-evaluation is not the solution, which is why the *procedure* of self-evaluation is a more robust focus for psychotherapy than maladaptive thoughts and self-esteem.[1] The key goal: freedom from rating the self.

Deep vs. Superficial?

Theorists of therapy often make a distinction between "deep" and "superficial" levels of the psyche. I see far fewer boundaries and far more fluidity between these so-called extremes. Indeed, once self-evaluation is the focus of therapy, it is hard to determine what is deep and what is on the surface. In practice that means that therapy must take into consideration a series or set of levels, starting from the outside and working in, more or less as follows:

- The larger society/culture (in this case, the market system)
- The client's personal world, including job, friends, relationships, etc.
- Family of origin

42 *Imaginary Sticks, Imaginary Stones*

- The internalized inner world (thoughts, world view, unconscious assumptions about reality)
- Identity (including self-evaluation aka opinion of self)

The focus on market-driven self-evaluation is actually a short-cut to the deeper levels of a client's psyche. What clients *think* about self is close to their hearts and often close to the heart of the matter—close, indeed, to their feelings and a great starting point for exploration.

Getting people to stop assessing themselves is often enough to improve their mood significantly. Often, though, recognizing the futility of self-evaluation is just the beginning of the work. For one thing, the struggle for high self-esteem often goes way back into childhood when negative identities, rooted in comparison and expectations of failure, first emerge. On top of that, the competitive nature of the market system makes (relative) failure particularly difficult to avoid, which reinforces the tendency to self-evaluate.

Finally, self-evaluation is insidious. It keeps coming back and it can apply itself to any trait, real or imaginary. Getting its tentacles to release may be one of the most time-consuming and frustrating aspects of therapy. Many clients even begin to evaluate themselves on the basis of how well they stop self-evaluating (see Chapter 7).

Here's a passage in which all the complicating factors appear together:

Cl: I live in a world that judges me all the time. My father judged me, now there are even people who are paid to judge me. They call them judges. Every time I go out into this world, I can win or lose a case. How can I stop thinking of myself as either a winner or a loser?

Th: Why? You win some, you lose some. You don't change each time. You're the same person.

Cl: I suppose. I've been trying to make that idea work for me, but it's tough going. For example, I used to evaluate myself on the basis of my other traits, my empathy, like you said. But then I realized that I was still rating myself. I can't stop. I even rate myself on how well I'm implementing the idea of not rating myself. It's insidious.

Th: This might help. Imagine that you had a child. That child would see you as Daddy. It wouldn't matter to the child if you won that day or lost that day. But it would matter if you were miserable and unresponsive.

Cl: So then I would be a good daddy or a bad daddy, wouldn't I?

The interventions described in this chapter do not, of course, apply to every case and every individual. They have been chosen to illustrate the

Imaginary Sticks, Imaginary Stones 43

connection between distress and the *outside* level—the market system. Certainly the market system is not the only cause of distress or the only target for psychotherapy. Therapists need to be just as sensitive as ever to all the other traditional sources of illness and misery. But this book is concerned with interventions that relate significantly to the character and consequences of the market system. Therapists will know how to go deeper.

The Elements of the Approach

In the following pages, the work has been broken down into separate elements. In an actual case, those elements don't necessarily present themselves in any particular order. As all therapists know, opportunities for intervention arise unpredictably. But I have often found that the order presented here seems to just happen, frequently. I am kind of attached to it and believe that if a therapist is on the lookout for it, good results will ensue.

Element One: Why Do You Have an Opinion?

This question is the key to everything that follows. Clients need to realize that self-esteem, high or low, is just an opinion—an opinion about oneself. Virtually every client comes in with an opinion about self and will sooner or later express it. The opinion, which takes many forms, can usually be reduced to a judgment or rating. More than likely, the rating fluctuates. Sometimes it's "I'm not good enough." Not good enough morally, professionally, socially, or in some other way(s). At other times, the rating is higher: "I'm actually OK." In some people, the rating goes up to "I'm really terrific."

It's necessary to allow clients to present their own opinion before making the intervention—before pointing out that they are expressing an opinion. The intervention is particularly effective if the client has already expressed both positive and negative opinions. Once that has happened, "why do you have an opinion?" can be followed with "can both those opinions be right?"

Clients often deny that what they've expressed is an opinion. They argue that it's actually a perception of reality. If they finally realize that it is just an opinion, they often try to convince me that their opinion is correct.

I don't try to counter their opinion. I don't try to bolster their self-esteem. Instead, I ask that odd question: "Why do you have an opinion (about yourself)?"

It would take a novelist to describe the surprise, shock, and disbelief that often run across the faces of the people who are asked the question. "Doesn't everyone?" is usually the first verbal response. Most clients come

44 *Imaginary Sticks, Imaginary Stones*

in believing that *everyone* has an opinion about self. "How can you not?" asked Roger. Here's a typical sequence:

Th: Well, tell me why you believe you're no good.
Cl: I haven't taken risks. I've stayed on the comfortable side. Comfortable job. Comfortable relationship. It's rather pitiful.
Th: Why haven't you taken risks?
Cl: I get scared when I think about it.
Th: What are you afraid of?
Cl: I'm afraid of failure.
Th: But you told me you knew that those Silicon Valley people have failed many times.
Cl: I know. That's what makes it so pitiful.
Th: So tell me what would happen if you failed.
Cl: I'm afraid my sense of myself would be affected.
Th: What do you mean by that?
Cl: I would have to change my view of myself.
Th: Your view of yourself.
Cl: Yes.
Th: Why do you have a view of yourself?
Cl: [stunned silence] Doesn't everybody?
Th: Not really.
Cl: Don't I need it to guide my behavior?
Th: Not really.

Evaluation: One's Self or One's Actions

Here, Roger introduces a key objection. Like many clients at this point, he's afraid that giving up his opinion of self will leave him without a moral compass. It needn't, and here's why: **There is a fundamental difference between assessing one's own value, on the one hand, and assessing the effectiveness and/or desirability of an action, on the other.**

Actions can be evaluated—deemed right or wrong, useless, useful, or self-defeating—without bringing in the value/worth of the self. In fact, bringing in the self is entirely unnecessary and not very useful. It is far more effective to judge one's actions as they affect others. That way, one can learn from one's mistakes. Compare these two responses:

1 "Oh, that didn't work. I'm a bad person."
2 "Oh, that didn't work. He was hurt. I shouldn't do that again."

It's easy, I think, to see that the second response is far more effective as a guide to the future than the first response. Conclusions about the self

Imaginary Sticks, Imaginary Stones 45

generally run into dead-ends. People can change what they do but not who they are.

Unfortunately, beliefs about the self are often twisted around action-oriented thoughts. That was the case with Alan, a high-level manager. Alan was barely aware of the difference between thinking about himself and thinking about what he needed to do. For him, *he* was often the problem. Before stating the need to do something, he would often interject the phrase "I want to do a good job at . . ." Or he would say: "I wonder if I'm doing a good job at telling people what they need to accomplish." Alan conflated "I need to do X to avoid a problem" with "it's my fault if there's a problem."

When therapy started, he argued that the two types of thinking were identical. We had to work on *separation and identification* before any progress could be made. Here are some suggestions that were made to Alan:

- Formulate actions plans without "I." Instead of "I need to . . ." use "What is needed here is . . ."
- Instead of focusing on possible bad outcomes (disasters) focus on the steps that need to be taken.
- Note the difference between these two types of thoughts.

Alan's response was slow. His mind kept telling him that the distinction I was making was artificial, so for many sessions he just kept arguing. Getting him to make the distinction became a big part of our work.

Here's another dialog. Notice how quickly the same theme surfaces:

Th: How are the breathing exercises going?
Cl: I get relaxed for a few minutes, but then the to-do list starts to come back and I lose track of the breathing.
Th: Your to-do list.
Cl: Yes.
Th: Why is that so intrusive?
Cl: There's a lot of stress at work.
Th: Actually, the stress isn't "at work." Stress is an individual's response to situations. Tell me what makes work so stressful for you?
Cl: I need to feel that I'm doing well, that I have some worth, that I'm a good person.
Th: So what you're really doing is trying to maintain your opinion of yourself.
Cl: I suppose so. Yeah. I guess you're right.
Th: Does that make sense to you?
Cl: Yes. I've always done it, as far back as I can remember.
Th: How far is that?
Cl: After college, I suppose.

46 *Imaginary Sticks, Imaginary Stones*

Th: Can you see that this procedure is contributing to your stress?
Cl: Very much so. But I have no idea how to stop doing it.

In extreme cases, opinion of self can actually undermine survival. Victoria came from a poor working class family, but she was both intelligent and seductive, a winning combination. She had married a wealthy man, a man with investments in various foreign countries. But she refused to take money from him. She continued to work at her low-paying job and insisted on paying her share of household expenses out of her own meager earnings. That decision kept her spending more or less at subsistence level. For one thing, it prevented her from getting proper medical care for her and her child. (She claimed that her husband was a notorious cheapskate who was happy with the arrangement, but I was not able to verify this for myself.)

I tried to understand her motivation:

Th: Why won't you take money from your husband?
Cl: I came from humble origins. He's from a well-to-do family. I don't want anyone to think that I'm a gold-digger.
Th: Really! What difference does it make what people think about that?
Cl: I guess it's really more what I think.
Th: I see. So you have an opinion about yourself—that you didn't marry for money—and you have to prove to yourself that you didn't.
Cl: Yes, it seems important.
Th: So important that you make decisions that affect your standard of living and that of your child on that basis.
Cl: It seems so.
Th: So you make decisions about your life in order to manage your own opinion about yourself.
Cl: I never actually thought of it that way.

Once she thought of it, Victoria was able to change her decision-making with relative ease.

Here's how Juan's father, a first-generation immigrant, responded when faced with the demands of the American economy:

Cl: My father's rule was 90%. Anything you do, he would say, do at least 90%. Anything less than that was no good. If I met that standard, I got everything I wanted. If I didn't, I was shut out. I was shut out often.
Th: How did that affect you?
Cl: I think I've been depressed ever since.

Juan's father had responded to the competitive society he found in America by creating arbitrary, rigid, and unrealistic "standards" for his son.

Imaginary Sticks, Imaginary Stones 47

As he grew up, Juan had naturally generated his own arbitrary standards and then proceeded to fail at them. "I have to be the best," he would say. But he regularly had to admit that he wasn't, because he tended to compare himself frantically to other people. Occasionally, though, if he got good grades in school, or, later, if he was successful at work, he would manage, for a little while, to believe that he was really good, really successful. Then, and only then, could he feel good. Therapy involved coming to realize that these standards were arbitrary and largely meaningless.

Vince's case illustrates how difficult it is for some people to overcome the tendency to compare. He was having trouble in the bedroom. Erectile failure. After some therapy, he actually discovered the reason. He was experiencing fear instead of arousal. He was comparing himself, in his mind, to other people—imaginary people. And, of course, he was seeing them as better lovers, so he feared his partner was judging him. It was clear that we needed to talk about comparison.

Th: Why do you compare?

Cl: Doesn't everybody? How do you not? I can't imagine it.

Th: Well, let's see if we can figure out how to imagine it. Some people, when they go window shopping, they just enjoy the items they see in the window. They don't even think about having them at home.

Cl: They don't want them? I can't imagine that.

Th: OK, try this. Imagine a walk in the country. You see a tree. Do you want to take it home?

Cl: Well, you can't take home a tree but I might think of building my house next to the tree.

Th: To possess it. I see. What about a sunset?

Cl: No different. I would think about having the colors at home, on a wall.

Th: So you are unable to see something without injecting yourself into the picture.

Cl: I guess not.

Th: And since you don't imagine that you are better than everyone at everything, you are worse than some and so you are insecure.

Cl: Yeah, it seems that way.

Th: So to overcome this, you would have to learn to imagine scenes and things and people without including yourself in the picture.

Cl: It certainly seems that way.

We had to spend considerable time, using meditation and trance work, helping Vince imagine without possessing and without inserting himself into the picture. Once he could do that, he was able to start learning sensory focus techniques (Kaplan, 1974) to keep his mind from wandering to himself and his world of imaginary competitors.

48 *Imaginary Sticks, Imaginary Stones*

Element Two: Recognize, Label, and Dismiss

Getting clients to realize that they are actually *doing* something when they engage in self-evaluation can be a problem. Clients often don't realize they are *doing* anything. They have the impression that they are simply registering, passively, an aspect of reality (their inadequacy; their value). They believe that they are noticing their inadequacy/value the way they might notice a sign on the street or a step on a stoop. They don't know that they are *creating* what they thought they were *noticing*, and thereby *causing* something—their own stress and/or misery.

Clients often have trouble getting over this hurdle. To do so, one has to be really clear on the difference between a thought and a perception. Simple examples can sometimes serve to illustrate the difference. "I have two arms and two legs" is a thought based on a perception. "The moon is made of green cheese" is a thought but not a perception—a thought with no connection to reality. "I am inadequate" is like "the moon is made of green cheese." It too is not a perception. But it masquerades as one and it feels like an insight.

One often gets an argument from clients who believe that they *are* inadequate. The point to be made, one way or another, is that there is no universally accepted standard for inadequacy and no measurement that can determine it. Inadequacy exists in the mind; it doesn't correspond to an objective category. There is no "adequate box" that one can get into or fall out of.

Once clients understand that their negative track is just a series of thoughts in their heads—no easy feat—the work begins. Here is a sequence which helps to avoid common obstacles and resistance:

- Recognize with "here it is again."
- Shift attention to the negative feelings in the body.
- Then, and only then, shift attention to something else, preferably something positive.
- Be prepared that it will take many repetitions (keep expectations down).

Clients must be warned of the difficulty. As stated before, the negative thoughts come back quickly at the beginning. Here's how Trish responded, early on: "I don't think I'm doing it right. Every time I try it, the thoughts come right back, and now it's worse. It's just another thing I'm failing at." Clients have to be reassured:

Th: The thoughts always come back right away when you first try it.
Cl: But it seems so simple. I should be able to do it.

Th: It *is* simple. But simple is not easy. Hitting a baseball is simple, but it's hardly easy.

Once clients have had some success, I try to congratulate them on having managed to overcome so successfully the hidden handicap of the negative voice.

On Thought-Stopping

Recognize, label, and dismiss may seem somewhat akin to *thought-stopping* but is actually quite different. Stopping a thought is difficult. In the past, when I talked about thought-stopping, I was often asked, with barely hidden sarcasm: "How in hell am I supposed to do that?" But *recognizing* a thought, if not easy, is nonetheless far easier than stopping one. Most people can learn to do it. They can be successful at it. It's a skill that can be practiced. It's an action, something to be done. Stopping a thought, on the other hand, is an outcome, something one must hope for.

Hopefully someone will run a controlled study showing that one technique is superior to the other.

Element Three: Separating Mood From Self-Evaluation

Thoughts vs. feelings. Success in therapy often depends on making a distinction, perhaps artificially sharp, between thoughts—what's in your head—and feelings, which are located in the body. The idea is that stinking thinking, as they say in AA, generally leads to bad feelings. Humans are capable of an infinite number of thoughts. There are only a few feelings (see Chapter 2 for a discussion of the emotions). They can usually be located in the chest or abdomen. Some people, mostly women, are aware of the actual sensations in the body. Others, usually men, either aren't aware of them or ignore them.

People will not give up self-assessment if their mood depends on wrenching their opinion of self into the positive zone. Here's an example (see "Bobo" in Chapter 10 for more work with this client, including this passage):

Th: How do you *feel* when you *think* you're terrific?
Cl: On top of the world, of course.
Th: Can you describe what you actually feel, in your body?
Cl: [long hesitation] Erect. Expansive. Really aware of surroundings.
Th: Energized?
Cl: Yes. Exactly!
Th: And when your opinion is low?

50 *Imaginary Sticks, Imaginary Stones*

Cl: Bent over. Tired. Like I'm being tied up.
Th: Constricted?
Cl: Exactly.
Th: Now you can see why you seek approval. It shifts your opinion and that changes the way you feel. It's like dope. In a sense you're addicted.

It follows that therapists must help clients make the sharpest possible distinction between an opinion and the mood that depends on it. When clients say they *feel* something, I first ask them *where* they feel it. This usually produces some surprise and confusion, followed by a fairly standard sequence:

Cl: What do you mean, where?
Th: In your body.
Cl: I don't know.
Th: Well, it's not in your toe, is it?
Cl: No. Somewhere in here, probably [waving their hands in front of their chest].
Th: Good. Could you point to the spot now?

Once location has been established, I ask them to describe *what* they are feeling. The most common answer is either depression or anxiety. I then ask them to translate their answer into actual physical sensations. (As all therapists know, depression is usually experienced as a weight, fatigue, and/ or hollow or empty sensation in the stomach area, while anxiety is usually experienced as increased heart rate, rapid breathing, and/or constriction in the chest.)

Eventually, this makes it possible for clients to have a stand-alone experience of mood—*mood independent of opinion*. Sometimes this is enough for them to understand the distinction and to start giving up having an opinion of self. Usually, though, it's necessary to keep asking "is that a thought or a feeling?" Clients gradually become more adept at making the distinction, and, as that happens, their mood tends to become more and more independent of their self-evaluation.

There is no good reason to make how one feels dependent on what one happens to be thinking about oneself. It makes one's mood too vulnerable. Any little setback can spin it into the doldrums; any success can send it flying off into space.

Here's a fairly typical case that illustrates the steps fairly well. Angelina worried constantly about disappointing others. She worried about disappointing her colleagues, her bosses, her friends, her parents, her extended

Imaginary Sticks, Imaginary Stones 51

family, and her husband. The worry was incessant enough to come to the attention of a colleague, who encouraged her to come to therapy. Here's how therapy proceeded:

Th: What happens if you disappoint someone?
Cl: I don't know. I imagine that they will feel bad.
Th: Then what happens?
Cl: I criticize myself.
Th: What do you say to yourself?
Cl: Thoughtless. Stupid.
Th: So it lowers your opinion of yourself.
Cl: Badly.
Th: How do you feel when you do that?
Cl: Do what?
Th: Say those things about yourself.
Cl: Bad. I feel bad.
Th: Can you describe the feeling?
Cl: [after several attempts] I think I'm a failure.
Th: That's a thought. What do you feel when you think you've failed?
Cl: [after several more attempts] I feel a sinking sensation in my stomach. And tightness . . .
Th: So what you feel is a response to what you think.
Cl: I guess so. I never thought about it.
Th: Do you see that [by avoiding disappointing others] you are actually managing your own opinion of you?
Cl: I guess so.
Th: Do you like thinking you're a failure?
Cl: No.
Th: Why do you keep thinking it?
Cl: You mean all I have to do is stop?
Th: I didn't say it was easy.
Cl: Doesn't sound like it.
Th: But if you stopped worrying about being a failure, you wouldn't feel those feelings . . .

Therapy then proceeded as described earlier, starting with recognize and dismiss.

In this case, Angelina was able to implement the tools almost immediately. She came back the next week and said that she hadn't been worrying about disappointing anyone and hadn't felt bad all week. "What should we talk about now?" she asked. We explored her childhood, relationships with parents and siblings, relationship with her life-partner, and any history of

52 *Imaginary Sticks, Imaginary Stones*

problems. Nothing. Angelina went off after a few weeks saying she would call if she had a recurrence. She didn't.

Success doesn't always come so easily. If I've given the impression that these interventions constitute a magical instant cure, I apologize. Many clients need time to digest and eventually implement the approach. With Dennis, for example, we had to go way back in time:

Cl: My wife left me a big mess the other day. It made me very anxious.

Th: Really? I would have thought you'd be angry.

Cl: Yeah, I'm angry at her, but I'm angry at myself too.

Th: Why is that? Did you contribute to the mess?

Cl: No, but if the apartment is in disorder, I take it as a sign that I don't have things together. You would say that it triggers my self-evaluation.

Th: That's a good catch.

Cl: Yeah, it reflects on me. Besides, someone might come over and think that I don't have things together.

Th: Why would you care?

Cl: I knew you were going to ask me that. I can't help it. I know we've worked on it again and again.

Th: It's hard, I know. Just try to tell me why.

Cl: It goes back to the self-worth thing. I know you say it's just an opinion, but I can't just be me. It doesn't seem good enough.

Th: And someone else's opinion can drive you to this place. Do you see how this makes you vulnerable?

Cl: [long silence] It goes back to wanting approval from my parents.

Th: All the way back there, huh.

Cl: I guess. I know I'm grown up now and shouldn't care.

Th: Hey, no shoulds. We've got to work it through. It takes time.

Cl: Forever?

Th: It just seems that way. Look at it this way. You're putting other people in the position of your parents. It isn't them anymore.

Cl: It just happens.

Th: Hey, I wonder. Are you doing that here?

Cl: Yes. I want you to think that I'm making progress.

Th: "You want me to think . . ."

Cl: Yes.

We had to catch him out many times before he began to relinquish his faith in self-evaluation.

Rodney also had worked hard to overcome his unhappiness. He was meditating regularly and he was catching his self-evaluation regularly. He felt OK on weekends and on vacation, but as soon as he returned to work

Imaginary Sticks, Imaginary Stones   53

he started to get depressed and anxious. He was beginning to think that the techniques wouldn't work for him.

Th: There's got to be something that brings you back to the misery.
Cl: I'm always disappointed.
Th: What are you failing at? No one is telling you you're failing.
Cl: I have an image in my mind and I can't let it go. If I stop hoping to realize that image, which happens for moments, it seems like there is no hope for me.
Th: What is the image?
Cl: It's a picture of how I'm supposed to be. I see myself doing things in a particular way. With ease and just right. As long as I believe that I'm doing things that way, I'm fine. But as soon as I realize that I'm not that way, everything goes bad.
Th: What does being that way mean to you?
Cl: It says I'm better than other people. Being better is everything. Any hint that I'm not better is depressing.

Clearly, then, the mere act of giving up self-evaluation can be felt as a powerful blow.

Treating the Symptom?

In one of our first sessions a client asked if I was just treating the symptom, waving vaguely toward my copy of the Norton edition of Freud's complete works:

Th: Not really. Or, perhaps better, not only. Think of it this way. The approach we're using actually constitutes a statement about reality. The statement is: There is no objective reality to your judgments. There is no "good" box you can get in. There is no "bad" box you have to get out of. There is no "special" box. When you pass these judgments on yourself, you are not naming a reality, you are not describing a reality, you are simply thinking a thought. So this approach actually defines or sets off reality from non-reality. It does far more than treat the symptom.

Marcello seemed satisfied. He stopped worrying about the treatment and started to work.

* * *

The next chapter presents some additional interventions aiming at neutralizing the acid of self-evaluation.

Note

1. The difference between the approach suggested here and standard approaches may seem slight but are significant. For example, the Anxiety and Depression Association of America recommends the following: "*Question the validity of your thinking and interpretations. When you recognize a lack of accuracy in what you are thinking, you are more likely to stop ruminating.*" This involves taking the questions you are asking as legitimate and rethinking your answers. I suggest that challenging the question is more effective.

6 Farther Out?

Some Additional Interventions

The interventions described in the previous chapter work well in many different kinds of therapeutic situations. The five interventions in the current chapter have a more limited application. Some of them are quite dramatic. They need to be introduced carefully. My practice is to do so only after a client has been taught a relaxation exercise and is able to produce a relaxation response (Benson, 1976).

The Five Interventions

1. *You Are a (Male/Female) Mammal*

Most clients pin their identity to high-level functions and traits. Asked who they are, they will most often say something along these lines: "I'm a good person" or "I'm a victim" or even "I'm not very talented." These types of response can best be understood as ratings: good enough, not good enough. A somewhat drastic way to overcome this self-evaluation is to focus on *what* we are instead of who we are.

Asked *what* they are, most people manage, after asking several times for clarification, to state that they are human. But if asked "what are humans?" the blank stare usually returns. With prompting, many people remember that in high school they learned that humans are mammals. Once the client is clear that humans are indeed mammals, the stage is set for a new identity: "I'm a male/female mammal." It's an identity that can't be rated. It just is.

One very tortured client then realized: "So I'm sort of a fancy monkey." Surprisingly enough, this barely understood sliver of identity was his first step on the road to recovery. An identity as a mammal takes a danger away— the danger of not being good enough.

At first most people find it hard to think of themselves this way. It insults their sense of specialness. So the intervention requires a lot of attention.

56 *Farther Out?*

One doesn't want clients to think they are "nothing but" a mammal, nor does one want them to conclude they are "just animals." They have to be steered toward a useful interpretation, to wit: *We are creatures, we are imperfect, we do not have to perform or excel to justify our existence.*

In my most self-evaluative moments, I had doubts about this intervention: Was it too big a jump? Could it be meaningful to people without an evolutionary perspective?

I got some reassurance when I read about what scientists call the "Copernican Principle," the idea that humans are not the measure of all things. Copernicus was, of course, the man who established that the earth was not the center of the universe. Civilization took a long time to absorb this idea, but it led to great intellectual and scientific progress. Individuals who grasp that they are not the center of the world also benefit enormously. They can relax a little and let go.

But I still sometimes worried that women in particular might find it demeaning. A recent exchange with a 45-year-old female client went a long way to easing my doubts. Natalie, a foreign-born client, thought of herself as a dancer. She wasn't a professional dancer but a woman who, like many others, had studied ballet in her youth and had tried for a career in ballet. The career was behind her but she still loved dancing. We happened to be talking about identity one day when out of the blue she offered that the identity of the Americans she knew was a mess:

> They have no feel for the body. They seem removed from it. They think of themselves as talking machines, maybe thinking machines. We dancers are identified with our bodies. They are part of who we are, not something irrelevant that we drag around because we have to.

Natalie's take on this confirmed my intuition that people need to identify with more than the fancy tricks the cerebral cortex can perform.

2. The Challenge: "Name Five Traits That Cannot Be Evaluated"

Asked to name five things about themselves that can't be evaluated, most clients flounder around helplessly without being able to answer. That's because their identity is attached only to the ideas they have about themselves: clever, nice, kind, good, reliable, etc., etc. No physical component of the organism figures in. But once they hit on "I am 5′6″" or "I have brown hair" they can go on to name the endless number of traits that make up who and what they are. This intervention helps clients form an identity that is not at the mercy of arbitrary judgments.

Farther Out? 57

Sometimes clients will argue that these other traits—the traits that can't be evaluated—are unimportant or inferior. When I'm in a bad mood, I'm tempted to respond somewhat harshly: "If you think that having two kidneys is not an important trait, wait until you have kidney disease." But being an experienced therapist, I make the point more gently.

3. You Are Not on Trial

As all therapists know, clients often describe having an inner dialog that resembles a trial. It's helpful to point out that it's a bizarre trial, one that Alice might have encountered in Wonderland, for the client is the prosecutor, the defense attorney, the judge, and the jury. He or she is scurrying around, amassing evidence, assessing it, arguing both sides of the case, and ultimately coming to a verdict—which can change at any time.

One way to bring home the absurdity of the procedure is to take first one side, then the other; first support the prosecution, then the defense. Here's an example:

Cl: I blew it. I should never have talked to my boss that way.
Th: That was quite damaging, wasn't it.
Cl: I never make the right decisions.
Th: You could have been much farther along in your career.
Cl: You bet. What's wrong with me?
Th: I don't know. Let's look for it. Remind me. You told me your boss was really out of line the other day when he chewed you out, didn't you?
Cl: Of course.
Th: Well, I can understand how you might have been upset.
Cl: Yeah, so?
Th: Maybe some part of you really did the right thing.
Cl: Do you think so?
Th: Well, isn't it possible?
Cl: I suppose so.
Th: Maybe there's a part of you that sees what's right and wants to do that and another part that just wants to do what is best for you.
Cl: I suppose.
Th: So it isn't a question of being good or no good, is it?
Cl: I guess not.
Th: Well you know, conflicting impulses are part of the human make-up . . .

If arguing both sides of the "case" is done subtly, clients will also shift their position. If accused, they will defend. If defended, they will accuse.

58   *Farther Out?*

Confronted with these contradictory opinions, clients often realize that the trial itself is absurd.

4.   *Exposing "Worth" and "Value"*

Many clients use "worth" and "value" to beat themselves up; their "objective" self-evaluation leads them to conclude they have neither. How does one undo such a belief? One way is to challenge the usefulness of these two terms:

Th: Did you ever think about the meaning of those words?

Cl: Naw, it's obvious.

Th: Well, maybe, but let's go into it. Do you believe that you are worth more or have more value than the grocer?

Cl: No. What do you take me for? I'm not one of those elitists.

Th: OK, I'm glad. Do you believe that the millionaire down the street is worth more than you?

Cl: Well, he's worth more money but he's not necessarily a better human being.

Th: OK, then. Let's look more closely at those two words. I think "worth" and "value" are like "ghost"; everyone knows what "ghost" means, but is there any such thing in the real world?

Cl: I don't believe in ghosts.

Th: Well, it seems to me you don't really believe in worth or value, either . . .

Arguments and examples like these can usually shake a client's faith in the validity of "value" and "worth."

The human species doesn't have a universal method of evaluating its members, but clients often believe there is one—one that judges them wanting. Money plays a role here. Money provides a standard, objective measure of value—of a sort. Measurement is appealing. It promises reliability, certitude. People want that, so they look for a non-monetary standard that promises to be equally objective. "Good," as in "good enough," is often what they hit on. They want to think they're "good" but they often end up falling short of that goal. So the struggle goes on.

5.   *Second-Guessing: "Costs and Benefits" vs. the Myth of the Best*

I have often found that clients who agonize about the self spend a lot of time second-guessing themselves. They are afraid to make mistakes. In part, this is because a mistake might have consequences in the external world, but often it's because a mistake would damage their self-image. Said Manny: "If I can't be sure it's the best decision I start beating myself up."

Th: Do you realize you're making a prediction? Are you a prophet?
Cl: How is that a prediction?
Th: Well, you can't know if it's the *best* decision until after you see the consequences and then compare to all the other possible decisions that you and anybody else could make.
Cl: I guess you're right. I never thought of that.
Th: Well, it's not an easy thought to get.
Cl: I don't actually have any information about the future so I couldn't know if a decision was best or not, could I?
Th: Right. But thinking about being the best seems to be very common in our society.
Cl: Yeah, there's so much competition.
Th: I think there might be a better way to think about decisions. It's right up your alley, really [Manny worked for a big Boston firm]. Why not think about costs and benefits of a decision, rather than trying to judge it.
Cl: Like we do at work.
Th: Right. Does that make sense?
Cl: I'll try it. Maybe.

Understanding that there are costs to every action can be very difficult for certain clients to accept; it goes against their grandiosity—their belief that they can be mistake-free. For that reason, the intervention can engender resistance and create anxiety, at least temporarily. It can even be taken to mean that the worst—the costs—will always happen. But in the longer run, getting rid of "best" and "worst" tends to reduce anxiety. Since costs can't be avoided, much less hangs on every decision. Much less is at stake (see Chapter 8 for more on anxiety).

Against Affirmations

The widely promoted technique of affirmation might seem to be a useful therapeutic technique, but I don't place much faith in it. First of all, affirmations are aimed at low self-esteem; they do nothing to counteract self-evaluation. Second, clients tend to discount affirmations: "You're just saying that because you're a therapist" or "I just don't believe myself when I say good things about me."

There is also research indicating that affirmations can, paradoxically, produce bad feelings (e.g. Wood et al., 2009). One client, call him Vincent,

60 *Farther Out?*

clearly writhed when receiving positive input. His immediate, visceral reaction was shame. He was actually aware of feeling flushed. He would get this feeling even when he made a good shot in golf. We eventually uncovered the reason. Vincent believed he was a fraud. He thought he fooled people and feared he would get caught.

Affirmations can sometimes help if a client has actually experienced very little positive input over the course of his or her life. But, for the most part, the best they can do is transform a negative self-representation into an oscillating self-representation. Affirmations will rarely enable clients to pin their self-concept in the high position.

Sometimes clients will respond to the idea that they needn't have an opinion of themselves with this objection: "Everybody says you have to believe in yourself, you have to have confidence, you have to pump yourself up. So how can you do this if you aren't supposed to think positively about yourself?"

The people who promote positive self-talk are correct in one sense; positive self-talk feels better than negative self-talk. But confidence is best gained from thinking less, not more, about the self. Thinking about the self simply strews doubt and hesitation along the path.

There is a state in which the self more or less disappears. It is found in many walks of life. Jazz musicians call it being in the groove. Athletes call it being unconscious. Eugen Herrigel (1953) found it in the art of archery. Zen monks seek to stay in it forever. Mihaly Csikszentmihalyi (1990) wrote a famous book about it; he called it *Flow*, the state in which the mind is focused *not* on the self, but on the action.

In these extreme instances, there are no thoughts about the self, no self-doubt and no fear. Such extraordinary states are rarely attained, but they point in the direction one needs to go to achieve quiet self-confidence and peace of mind.

* * *

The next chapter continues the overview of self-evaluation, its effects, and its treatment.

7 Some Sad Bedfellows of Self-Evaluation

When one takes self-evaluation as a focus, a number of puzzling behaviors begin to make sense. Some of them will be illustrated in this chapter.

Attachment to the Negative Track

The negative track doesn't give up easily. Strange as it might seem, individuals often cling to their self-hatred. A variety of factors contribute to this phenomenon. We'll deal with each one in turn.

Pre-Suffering

"If I anticipate a bad outcome," said Justin, "it won't feel so bad when it actually happens." Clients often call this "preparing for the worst-case scenario." I call it pre-suffering—suffering before anything bad has happened. Clients often believe that pre-suffering is an effective way to prepare for bad outcomes. In practice this "strategy" means that the individual suffers over and over before anything bad has happened.

It's generally necessary to challenge the usefulness of pre-suffering as a procedure. Simply pointing out how much more suffering pre-suffering actually creates can help.

Th: Is it really worth it to you to re-experience all that anxiety every time?
Cl: I don't think I ever factored that in.

It's also useful to point out that by pre-suffering, clients are defending themselves against *their own emotions.*

Th: What are you preparing yourself for?
Cl: I've never asked myself that question.

62 *Some Sad Bedfellows of Self-Evaluation*

Th: OK, think about it now. You're arming yourself, steeling yourself. What against?

Cl: I guess it's against what I would feel?

Th: So you're protecting yourself against your own emotions?

Cl: I guess so. That doesn't seem necessary, does it?

Th: No, but until this moment, you haven't had a choice. Now we can work on catching it and cutting off the anxiety.

Cl: Sounds good.

Th: Why do you think you became afraid of your own feelings?

And so we continued with that exploration.

The absurdity of the procedure can often motivate a client to fight against it. But one has to be prepared for agitated responses. Said Benny: "Not prepare for the worst? You're crazy if you think I'm going to risk being overwhelmed."

Fear of Losing Motivation

When presented with the idea of giving up negative self-evaluation, some clients express a strange fear: "You're going to take away my motivation." That was Andy's response, and he had a point. He had scrambled all his life to avoid becoming what he feared he might be— inadequate. He was motivated to get ahead because he feared falling behind, a fear the market system reinforces. Negative self-evaluation *was* his motivation. He brought evidence in support of it and he reasoned convincingly.

This "motivation" is apparently an inner sense of urgency, a desperate need to stay ahead of the ominous specter of failure. The urgency leads to a twin compulsion—work and worry. The prolonged anxiety can, of course, lead to depression, especially when failure, relative or otherwise, looms. Therapy involves getting at the root of the self-evaluation—the cognitive-emotional black hole at the center of identity.

Here's another version of the same problem. Cramden had been unemployed for months but he was not doing what he thought he should be doing to protect his family. He was trying to get himself to act by criticizing himself:

> I haven't been applying for as many jobs as I should. I have a friend who's taken up the flute now that he has time. I want to do so many things. I want to play more music. I want to meditate. There are two books I really want to read. I don't do any of it. I watch TV and stare off into space. I don't like the person I am.

Some Sad Bedfellows of Self-Evaluation 63

Cramden was not comfortable when I failed to encourage his self-criticism.

Clearly we had to address the practical issue first. He did need a job, and he hadn't been assiduous; he had been submitting applications no more than once a week. So we created a plan that included his wish-list: every day, including weekends, he was to meditate for 10 minutes and then apply for one job, but only one. After that, his assignment was to consider himself completely free to do anything he wanted.

After establishing the plan, we went to work on his resistance:

Th: You've been trying to motivate yourself to be who you should be by criticizing who you are. That won't work.

Cl: Why can't it?

Th: You're confusing what you should be with what you want to be. You spin back and forth between those two different things. You're getting overwhelmed.

Cl: But I can't keep on doing nothing, like this.

Th: Of course not. You're going to follow the plan, and once you've applied for one job, for the rest of the day, you will do whatever you fancy, whether you think it's valuable or not.

Cl: I don't think I can do that.

At this point, I suggested some trance work. After a few minutes of deep breathing and silence, I dropped in the following suggestion: "You have to accept yourself as you are."

His answer was a long time coming:

Cl: But I can't afford to continue like this. I have to do something.

Th: Has criticizing yourself all day the way you are doing helped?

Cl: No, but what's the alternative?

Th: Think about the way alcoholics introduce themselves at AA meetings.

Cl: "I'm an alcoholic."

Th: Right. You are who you are. You have to start from where you are. *You* are the person who sometimes chooses to watch TV when he could be doing something more respectable. *You* are the person who'd rather not send in endless applications for jobs you don't want or jobs you can't get. Stop pretending to be someone else.

Cl: I am who I am.

Th: Right. And you're not going to become someone else, by reading or playing or worrying or hoping. But you can *do* some things differently, and now you have to, so let's increase the application rate and let's do some meditation and then let's just be who we are. [after a considerable period of quiet] Come back now.

64 *Some Sad Bedfellows of Self-Evaluation*

Cl: [wiping his brow] Actually, I feel much better. Like a weight is gone.
Th: OK, that's good. We don't need weights. Life is hard enough.

Fear of Emptiness

"What will I think about if I stop trying to make myself better?" asked Joe. This "fear of emptiness" may be fairly rare, but it too can sustain attachment to the negative self.

A lot of exploration is usually needed at this point because the reasons why a mind is so dominated by self-oriented thoughts may be obscure. Ultimately therapy has to focus on helping the client to find something of equal or greater interest. That can be difficult. Said Joe: "I'm sorry but nothing is as fascinating as my self. It's so complex, so intricate." Encouraging clients to think about what they want, rather than how good they are, is generally helpful. Eventually, clients freed from the tyranny of self-absorption find other things to think about, but the transition doesn't always go smoothly.

Hidden Grandiosity, Specialness, and Identity

For some of the afflicted, one of the most addictive features of negative self-evaluation is its ability to make one "special." "Especially bad" is still special whereas just OK is ordinary, drab, and ultimately depressing. Let Audrey tell it. "I don't want to be like everyone else. I want to be different. At least if I'm bad, I'm different." Audrey didn't know that in America, the craving to be special is rather widely shared, at least in part because the market system prizes specialness so intensely.

There is a key point that one can make to undermine this kind of specialness: *One person's negative track is just like every other person's negative track. There's nothing special about any of them.* I often make the case this way: "If one could print out, directly from the brains of a group of depressed people, each person's negative track, most people wouldn't be able to recognize their own printout." This idea tends to be disconcerting to those who are hanging on to their specialness. Some are downright sarcastic. "I thought you were supposed to make me feel better," said one. He was going to have to wait.

The "hidden" in hidden grandiosity is often a serious obstacle, as Xavier's case illustrates. You can't give up what you don't know is there. Xavier had spent some time working on his disaster scenarios when the following conversation took place:

Cl: I know you don't think so but they [the disasters] do seem likely, because of my shortcomings.

Some Sad Bedfellows of Self-Evaluation 65

Th: My guess is you keep getting a powerful negative sensation every time you realize that you have shortcomings.

Cl: Yes.

Th: It comes as a shock each time.

Cl: Yes. Each time.

Th: This seems kind of grandiose to me.

Cl: What do you mean?

Th: Part of you seems to think that you shouldn't have any shortcomings.

Cl: I never thought of that. I suppose it's true . . .

Th: Suppose we reframe "shortcomings" as "imperfections." Do you think you shouldn't have imperfections?

Cl: It's very hard for me to accept that I have imperfections. I immediately start to work on getting rid of them.

Th: So you can be perfect.

Cl: It seems silly when you put it that way.

Xavier wasn't able to relinquish the negative view of himself until he had brought his grandiose self to light.

Hidden or manifest, grandiosity's charm is perilous, because it brings the negative along with it. Rodolfo, a university instructor, came in because of anxiety. "I have too many things to do. Reports, articles, lectures, students. It's endless." He reported that he was getting it all done, and had been for years, but could not shake the feeling. I asked him to tell me exactly why having so much to do was making him anxious, given that he was so successful. "What do you mean?" he first said. "It's natural to worry". It took some weeks to get beyond that, but he finally came up with what turned out to be the answer: "When I imagine not being able to finish it all, I start to think badly of myself." That, of course, brought us right to the uselessness of self-evaluation, and thence to "Why do you have an opinion?"

The conversation went along roughly as usual until I brought up the idea that positive self-evaluation might be as bad as the negative:

Cl: That can't be true.

Th: Why not?

Cl: When I think highly of myself, I feel good about myself. I don't want to give up that feeling. If I don't feel good about myself I feel bad and I don't like that.

Th: So the only way you know to feel good is to have a high opinion of yourself.

Cl: Right. How else?

Th: Well, why can't you have a good feeling just because you succeed at something, or just because you get something you wanted?

66 *Some Sad Bedfellows of Self-Evaluation*

Cl: It doesn't seem to work.

Th: So you're addicted to this one thought. It's your junk, your fix, your own personal opioid.

Cl: I never thought of it that way.

Therapy consisted of weaning Rodolfo from his addiction.

"Imperfection IS immoral." This unusual statement emerged from a conversation with Rafe about hidden grandiosity. He was aroused and adamant:

Cl: If I make a mistake, it's an indication that something is wrong with me. Otherwise, how would I ever correct a mistake?

Th: There are many reasons to correct a mistake or to vow never to do it again. You don't have to criticize yourself to do it. You just have to look at the consequences.

Cl: If I trip and fall down, doesn't that say something about me?

Th: I don't think that's a good example. Suppose you're making change and you give a dollar too much. Wouldn't you have an incentive to avoid that mistake in the future?

Cl: I have a hard time separating the two. When I make a mistake, *I* did it. There's a problem with *me*.

Th: I think we're back to hidden grandiosity. If you weren't thinking that you're perfect or supposed to be perfect, then the realization that you've made a mistake wouldn't produce negative emotions. It's only because of grandiosity that mistakes generate so much painful emotion.

Cl: It'll take me awhile to put that into practice.

The Desire to Be Different

The desire to be different is often but not always related to hidden grandiosity. Most people, at least in the market system, gravitate to *difference* when they define themselves; they look for what (they hope) makes them unique. If they can't think of anything positive, they will embrace the negative, often with a sense of pride: "At least I don't have any illusions about myself" is commonly heard. In such cases, it can be useful to propose *similarity to others* as a basis for identity: "It's just us humans here."

Often, clients have never considered this option because the assumption, that identity has to be based on difference, had been automatically incorporated into their identity long before they had a chance to think about it. It's just another feature of the market system. It is often helpful to point out that thinking about similarity promotes human contact, connection, and belonging, all of which have a certain appeal to clients who are alone or lonely.

Some Sad Bedfellows of Self-Evaluation   67

Fidelity to a Parent's Message

Diana had a particularly bad case of attachment to the negative track. Like Juan, she was the daughter of immigrants who were shaped by their encounter with the American market system. Her mother had raised her to believe that being the best was the only thing worth being. Nothing else interested or motivated her. So, despite being an accomplished professional with artistic abilities, Diana lived in a world devoid of color and interest:

Cl: What's the point of anything if you can't be the best?

Th: None of your accomplishments mean anything to you?

Cl: What? I make a living, I play the piano for friends, what's the good of that?

Th: Do you think that this has anything to do with your mother's messages?

Cl: So what if it's my mother who told me. It's still true, isn't it?

Th: I'm sure she believed it.

Cl: She was right, wasn't she?

Th: Well, lots of people don't believe it and are living happy lives, aren't they?

Cl: Yes. They delude themselves. I can't.

Th: Do you think people in your country of origin believe this too?

Cl: Perhaps not. They are peasants. What's to learn from them?

Th: What if we look at the effect of your mother's message rather than its truth or falsehood?

Cl: What effect?

Th: Your unhappiness.

Cl: How is that related?

Th: You see no value in anything because of your self-evaluation: "Not the best."

Cl: That's self-evaluation?

Th: Yes, of course. And you're attached to putting yourself down. You swear by it. You don't want to give it up.

Cl: I don't know how.

Diana had never actually challenged her mother's message, nor had she connected it with the desolation of her life. Her "failure" was simply a fact of her life. It took her some time to get on board with a therapy that wasn't based on that "fact." For one thing, she had to confront her reluctance to believe that her mother could be wrong. Eventually, though, she managed to start taking pleasure in the little things of life.

68 *Some Sad Bedfellows of Self-Evaluation*

Cultural Identity

For Ron, self-assessment was a cultural trait, an essential part of being Jewish:

Cl: We think about things. We agonize over them. We question our motives. It's what we do. I wouldn't recognize myself if I didn't.

Th: Do you have to conclude that there's something wrong with you?

Cl: If we didn't, how would we know that we weren't fooling ourselves and just making ourselves feel better? Just justifying?

Th: What if you just judged actions, not your self? Wouldn't that get around the problem?

Cl: I don't know. I never made the distinction.

Ron spent weeks trying to convince me that he really was inferior. Only then did he start to work at giving up that rather self-defeating belief. It did not go easily. To him, it felt that he was giving up his identity. We had to re-anchor him in his other cultural practices before he could let go.

Some Other Consequences of Self-Evaluation

An Army of Imposters

I sometimes wonder if all Americans believe they are frauds. The belief pops up in therapy all the time. The afflicted believe that their achievements are fake. They are sure that they have fooled everyone, including bosses, friends, and lovers. The belief seems most prevalent among clients who are acutely aware of their own doubts, the mistakes they almost made, the better moves they might have made, and possibly the bluffing they have engaged in. Their self-awareness leads them to carry around an identity that is permanently stained.

It's important to note that this condition is really only possible when identity is based on achievement rather than on belonging. People often pretend to be more *competent* than they are, but unless they have a serious mental illness or are employed as a spy, they don't generally pretend to belong where they don't.

Here is a sequence that often leads to productive work with imaginary frauds:

Th: Can you see that this is your opinion of yourself?

Cl: Well, no, not really. It's reality, actually, not my opinion.

Th: No doubt about it?

Some Sad Bedfellows of Self-Evaluation 69

Cl: No, not really.
Th: Has anyone ever expressed a different view?
Cl: Yes [sheepishly], but I think I fooled them.
Th: So there were many?
Cl: Yes. I suppose so.
Th: You fooled all those people?
Cl: I think so.
Th: You must be pretty smart, then . . .

One way to undermine this conviction is to point out how grandiose it is. Ella, who had recently landed a job at a major consulting firm, thought she had fooled her Harvard Business School professors and her supervisors at work:

Th: So how did you manage?
Cl: I don't know. I don't understand why they didn't see through me at school, and it beats me why the people at my company don't either.
Th: You must be pretty clever then.
Cl: What do you mean?
Th: Well, those are pretty smart people, aren't they?
Cl: Sure.
Th: Doesn't that make you smarter?
Cl: Huh. [long hesitation] That never occurred to me.
Th: Really? Not even a glimpse?
Cl: Well, now that I think of it, I did wonder some time, but that idea didn't stay around.

Once Ella was able to confront the grandiosity, she started to let go of her self-denigration. The imposter syndrome eventually went with it.

It's worth noting that occasionally a client will terminate when pressed too insistently to give up the negative track. I have learned to curb my enthusiasm.

More on the Perils of High Self-Esteem

We've talked about these perils in several places but self-esteem is so central to self-evaluation that the topic deserves extra space. High self-esteem has, of course, traditionally been the antidote for low self-esteem. It *feels* better, which is obviously why people seek it. But in a sense, high self-esteem, like dope, is addictive. And, like any addiction, it has some serious drawbacks.

The search for the high locks people into the need for ego-boosting approval. Few people manage, by themselves, to fix their self-evaluation

70 *Some Sad Bedfellows of Self-Evaluation*

in the high position, so they twist themselves into knots to get the approval they require.

High self-esteem is all about self. Searching for it promotes interest and involvement in the self. The search does not serve any social purpose and doesn't necessarily promote the interests of the person engaged in it.

The search itself often produces oscillating self-representation. As described in Chapter 5, people who criticize themselves are often on a more or less subconscious mission to prove that they are at least OK. They marshal evidence in favor of the positive view of themselves, but they get submerged, regularly, in waves of the negative. Indeed some people manage to sustain, almost simultaneously, two incompatible views of themselves.

As is well-known, oscillating self-representation is a feature of some serious syndromes, including borderline personality organization (Kernberg, 1975), but it exists in milder form, and as this book indicates, I believe the milder form owes something to the extremes of reward and failure that characterize the market system (see Chapters 2, 3, and 4).

The word "oscillating" might convey an orderly procession, a stately march of thought and mood across the span of days and weeks. What actually happens is often a swirl of thoughts and images tearing at the mind like scrap metal in a tornado. The conflicting self-representations can flash almost simultaneously, leaving the individual confused and unable to focus.

Joan had a relatively serious case of the mild form; perhaps she was what one might call a borderline borderline. For several weeks, she had expressed nothing but self-criticism. Her mind was constantly badgering her about her faults. She was struggling with the idea of "worth"; she didn't think she had any. These thoughts brought on waves of negative emotion. She felt terribly lonely, even though she now had friends and a lover. She had her own definition of loneliness: "Loneliness means not getting the recognition you think you deserve from others."

She eventually revealed that to counter the negative self-image, she indulged in a secret fantasy: "I imagine that I'm a gifted actress. I'm admired by everyone. I'm invited everywhere. I win award after award." This was, of course, a grandiose self-image—and a typical market-system dream.

Joan saw the possibility of extraordinary success in the system as the solution to her problems. The euphoria of this fantasy was the state she sought, desperately, to be in. She mourned it when she wasn't in it. She reveled in it when she could bring the picture to mind, but any little setback threw her back into the worthless box. Encouraging her to think highly of herself would have been playing into the success fantasy.

Joan had been born into a competitive world but she wasn't equipped to deal with it. Her troubles had started early. She was bullied in childhood and was still having traumatic memories of it. Her parents, unsuccessful

Some Sad Bedfellows of Self-Evaluation 71

people themselves, hadn't known how to protect her. Her father left early in her life. She didn't date in the often vicious microcosm of high school. She continued to feel like an outsider in college despite a few affairs. In later life, she experienced a series of rejections by the men she was attracted to.

Therapy had to help her give up both of her damaging self-representations. She had to understand that the grandiose image was as destructive as the negative one. I first defined both of Joan's self-representations as "opinions." Once she could see that they were, we went to: "Why do you have an opinion?" As usually happens, that caught her by surprise. Like most people, she had never asked herself the question. We had to wrangle about it for several sessions.

Once we had agreed that her problems were in her head, Joan began to recognize and label the self-evaluative thoughts. But she soon ran into a thought/feeling problem. Confronting her negative self-assessment tended to trigger more waves of negative emotion; seeing her ideal self as merely an opinion created an acute sense of loss.

Once Joan developed some familiarity with her mind, I introduced the sequence described in previous chapters: recognize and label; shift to the attendant emotions; then shift to something else, preferably a pleasant activity.

Naturally, I warned her to be aware of the difficulty: "The thoughts will come back quickly when you first start to fight them. Be aware that they are insidious. Your mind will start to evaluate how well you are doing the exercise."

After a few sessions, we started to explore, in very light trance, the incidents of rejection that continued to trouble her. I frequently brought the discussion around to her two self-representations and to her hope that material success would solve all her problems. Joan eventually recognized that her desperate drive to succeed was also a drive to create an acceptable identity. At that point, she was able to see that what she had to achieve *was* the identity—a relatively stable one—rather than success in the outside world. And so the work began.

The Enhancement of Guilt

The proper domain of guilt is the action: "I did a bad thing; I feel bad." As argued previously, when applied to identity, instead of to an action, the power of guilt is magnified. People who believe that they've committed reprehensible acts often, if not always, believe that they are bad people. Often, the bad things they've done come back to haunt them in waves. When they remember the reprehensible act, they remember that they are *not good*.

72 *Some Sad Bedfellows of Self-Evaluation*

It's helpful to remember that under current conditions, guilt can be as anachronistic as fight or flight. Fight or flight was a useful response to a rustling in the bush, for example; a lion might lurk there. It's somewhat less useful when triggered by a boss's frown. Guilt, as pointed out in Chapter 2, was a useful survival mechanism when humans lived in bands and depended on relatives for survival. Guilt tended to keep our ancestors in line at a time when staying on the good side of the group was the only way to survive. Guilt is less useful when mild disapproval, even from strangers, can trigger depression.

It goes without saying that guilt, like fear, can, in some situations, be adaptive and useful. People have to avoid committing crimes, stealing from friends, and betraying loved ones. But aside from one convicted murderer, I rarely encounter clients who have actually done anything that would condemn them to a life of self-hatred. Therapists have to deal with guilt sensitively but should keep in mind that most often, clients exaggerate the severity of their misdeeds, the degree of harm they have done, and the amount of punishment they deserve.

* * *

In the next chapter, we'll look more closely at the connection between self-evaluation and anxiety.

8 A Little More on Anxiety

Freedom is great but problems come with it. A common drawback of life in a system where one's position is *not* forever defined by history, tradition, family, and class is a constant feeling of anxiety about one's place in the world. Democracy, and its handmaiden, the market system, is such a system. In it, one's place is up for grabs. A lot is at stake, a lot of the time.

As we've seen, the connection between negative self-evaluation and depression is obvious: If people really believe they're not good enough, they're going to feel bad. *Not good enough* is a quintessentially depressing belief. The connection between negative self-evaluation and anxiety is somewhat less self-evident. It generally goes something like this: "If I'm not good enough, then how can I deal successfully with whatever comes up—with threats and danger, and, for that matter, with opportunity?"

Throughout this chapter, keep in mind the discussion of pre-suffering in Chapter 7. Labeling anxiety pre-suffering often drains some of the fear and opens the way for clients to start dealing with their concerns. Keep in mind also that if people have doubts about self, they are likely to be anxious about the future. Finally, it goes without saying that some form of relaxation training is essential when treating anxiety.

Planning vs. Worrying

A young client, call her Julie, was having trouble grasping the difference between planning and worrying. Needing to define the difference, I came up with this: "Planning is about an *action* you can take or a *decision* you can make. Worrying is about an *outcome* you are imagining."

The distinction is important. Thinking about outcomes tends to be helpless thinking. Thinking about a decision tends to promote a sense of agency.

Disaster scenarios are about outcomes. Real disasters can happen. Disasters truly loom if the environment is dangerous and/or if the support system is weak. But in a market system, people run disaster scenarios when the only

74 *A Little More on Anxiety*

looming disaster is the possible loss of a potential payoff. In other words, *not maximizing* a payoff becomes a disaster. When potential payoffs are high, the consequences of not doing the "right" thing or making the "best" move are particularly upsetting, so a lot appears to be at stake.

By regularly asking, "Is there a decision you have to make?" a therapist can often pry thinking away from outcomes and disasters and onto decisions and actions.

Here's a sample of how therapy with Julie proceeded:

Th: What decision do you have to make now?
Cl: I have to decide which job to take.
Ch: And what are you worrying about?
Cl: Where I'll be in five years. Ten years. I'm not sure.
Th: Is there any way you can tell which job would put you ahead then?
Cl: Not really.
Th: Then you have to decide on some other basis.
Cl: But won't the decision have outcomes?
Th: Probably, but you don't have information about the outcome, so shift your attention to something you can do something about. Bring your thinking back to the present.

Once Julie could recognize a disaster scenario she could start to plan rather than worry.

A Perfect Life

Another young client, call him Bruce, wanted to live the perfect life, a vision that shimmers in the distance when a society proclaims that "anything is possible" and asserts that "you can be all that you can be." Bruce believed in the vision and therefore felt compelled to avoid mistakes. Every mistake was a disaster that meant he wasn't what he thought he was. As a result, he was unable to decide on a path for his life. He was stymied, unable to act.

Th: What if there is *no* right or best move? Or at least, no way to know?
Cl: Then I'm really screwed.
Th: What if you thought in terms of costs and benefits rather than mistakes? Everything you do will have some costs and benefits.
Cl: I have to accept costs?
Th: Of course. Everybody does, all the time. There are no alternatives that don't have costs.
Cl: I've always tried to find the solution that doesn't have any.

Th: That must be frustrating.
Cl: You aren't kidding. I weigh and weigh and end up nowhere.

Bruce had to realize that his procedure—trying to find the "right" answer—was faulty. He had to learn to think in terms of costs and benefits (see Chapter 6). Right vs. wrong is often a consequence of having too many options—which in turn is a characteristic of systems with freedom and big payoffs. Once right/wrong is eliminated, many of the unrealistic options fall off the table. As they fade, so do the disasters.

Is the "Best" the Worst?

George also came in complaining of anxiety. He eventually revealed that he agonized fruitlessly about every decision and every contingency. "I always try to make the best possible decision. Even crossing a street, I think about the best way to turn. I'm very competitive. Even with myself."

Th: So there's always something at stake? In every decision?
Cl: Yeah. It's my nature.
Th: And you wonder why you are prone to anxiety?
Cl: [long hesitation] You know what? I think we've hit on the underlying root.

After introducing relaxation training and discussing the irrationality of this behavior, I went back to George's statement about his nature:

Th: You know, it might be your nature, but I think rather it might be more a product of this society. If you think about it, the values you are talking about are the values of a competitive economy. "Always do the best you can." "Compare yourself to others, beat them out."
Cl: Sure. That's the way I was trained. It never occurred to me that there was a problem.
Th: OK. Now that you can see that there *is* a problem, we can begin to work on it.

The Terror of Disappointing

"I come to the office early. I agonize over every customer's problems. I answer every phone call within seconds, even late at night."

Jimmy was compulsively trying to ward off disasters by pleasing everyone. His terror had produced irritable bowel syndrome (IBS), so he was living in fear of being cut off from a toilet.

76 *A Little More on Anxiety*

Th: Do you think needing to please might have anything to do with your symptoms?

Cl: I can't help it. I'm miserable if people are unhappy with me.

These attributions about himself got in the way of making any progress on his IBS. When we first made the connection between his symptoms and his beliefs, he clearly got frightened: "I'm not sure it's worthwhile making changes to my lifestyle, even if it improves the symptoms." We had to keep walking through his daily routines until he realized that his whole life was controlled by his beliefs.

Therapy proceeded in two relatively long phases. In the first phase, Jimmy realized that he was dependent on the happiness of others to feel good:

Th: Why do you care if they aren't happy?

Cl: I don't know.

Th: Well then, tell me what happens to you if they aren't happy.

Cl: I get miserable.

Th: So your mood depends on what you think about the happiness of others.

Cl: Of course.

Th: What about *your* happiness? What do you want?

Cl: That hardly occurs to me. I don't really know.

We went on to develop his hopes and desires for himself. Jimmy eventually came to realize that his dependence was a result of his having an opinion of self that he had to protect:

Th: So if you don't make them happy, you wouldn't be you?

Cl: Right. That's who I am.

Th: Did you ever wonder why you have that opinion?

Therapy then proceeded along the lines described in Chapter 5. Jimmy eventually developed a more balanced view of life. He joked with me a lot about being a mammal (see Chapter 6). When he disagreed with me, he would roar and say "I wish I was a lion."

The Spin

Colin, who had already done some work on his negative track, came in one day complaining about a phenomenon which at first he had a hard time explaining. "Now that my self-criticism has quieted down, I seem to have more time to think about things, but now everything is crowding in on me all at once. I've been having trouble prioritizing."

A Little More on Anxiety 77

This, of course, was the spin, a stampede of thoughts and images that follow after each other with no pause and no interruption. Before any one of them can be dealt with, another comes crashing along, often leaving the victim feeling overwhelmed and helpless. The spin, we discovered, was what had been causing Colin to stare off into space while people, especially his wife, were talking to him.

While the spin may be a feature of anxiety in all cultures where anxiety is known, the characteristics of the market certainly contribute to it. Start with the endless choices, the competing demands of work and home, the expanded sense of personal responsibility, the agendas of others, the cult of efficiency (the *best* way), and the urgencies of profit and status. Add what you like to the list.

I usually start by walking clients through all their responsibilities and entanglements. Simply identifying the items on the list often helps to slow the spin down. Next we go through what clients think is at stake in each case—disasters, payoffs, opportunities, etc.

In the short run, this process can actually increase anxiety, as the client's conscious mind begins to contemplate the seemingly monumental tasks ahead. However, as clients begin to recognize disaster scenarios for what they are, the anxiety goes back down to baseline. Then treatment can proceed in standard fashion.

Colin was taught to meditate. After a week, he reported that he was recognizing the spin "from a different vantage point. I'm above it, looking down on it." By the next week he could control it by selecting one item from it and doing something about that one item. This was an unusually successful result for one week.

As a next step, Colin was instructed to stop prioritizing:

Th: It wastes time. You can spend hours prioritizing.
Cl: What? Everyone says you have to prioritize.
Th: How is that working for you?
Cl: Not well, but I thought it was because I was doing it wrong.
Th: All the time you spend prioritizing, you don't get anything done. Instead, just pick anything out of the spin and deal with it. Take it off the to-do list. You'll get a lot done.
Cl: But what if there's a deadline?
Th: If there's a real deadline, imposed from outside, you'll notice. Generally you only have to prioritize, through your own efforts, if there is no obvious deadline.

Prioritizing, which is so often presented as a solution, is often just another word for spinning. It's better to get something off the to-do list, enjoy a sense of accomplishment, and have one thing less to do.

78 *A Little More on Anxiety*

Most people actually work better with deadlines. If someone is missing deadlines, the problem goes deeper than prioritizing.

The Sneakiness of the Spin

The spin can be difficult to spot. It can start with something perfectly neutral, like a memory of a place one happens to have been that day. Then, by a series of steps—something you said there, something said to you, a memory of a similar time or place—you can find yourself, all of a sudden, in the midst of an agonizing self-appraisal, thinking of all the terrible things you've done, all the terrible things that have happened to you, or all the terrible things that could happen to you. The apparently harmless start can happen when you least expect it, even if you have already learned to recognize the heart of the spin itself. If this is happening to clients, they will have to advance awareness still another step; they will have to learn to recognize the very first steps and catch the direction of the associations. Not an easy task.

Anxiety as Both Carrot and Stick

For Pierre, it turned out that anxiety had been, in his mind, essential to his success. I discovered this when I made the following more or less standard observation:

Th: If you're thinking about doing something or not doing it, or how to do it, you're thinking about something useful. If you're worrying about how it will all come out in the end, you're probably wasting your time.

He came back with this:

Cl: The problem is, if I'm not anxious about something, I don't do anything about it. It just fades into the background. I don't have any incentive to do it.
Th: So if you're anxious, you have an incentive.
Cl: Right.
Th: Doesn't that mean you live life as if you're on the edge of a precipice?
Cl: Yes, exactly. Very uncomfortable. But what can I do?
Th: It seems absolutely essential?
Cl: Yes.
Th: [after a long hesitation] Tell me, then, do you sometimes suspect that you're not good enough [for the position you hold]? You have to think about everything you do otherwise you will fail? Get fired?

A Little More on Anxiety 79

Cl: Yes, exactly.
Th: So sometimes you think that you *are* OK and sometimes not.
Cl: Yes, exactly.
Th: Let's see now, do you realize that thinking you are good enough is an opinion?
Cl: I suppose so.
Th: And not being OK is also an opinion, right?
Cl: Right.
Th: All right. Tell me this. If your opinion was that you should get the Nobel Prize, would that opinion convince anyone to give it to you?
Cl: No, of course not.
Th: So then would your negative opinion of yourself help persuade someone that you're not doing a good job?
Cl: No, not really.
Th: So tell me. Why do you have an opinion?

We went on to develop the stress-relieving implications of not trying to be the judge of oneself.

Identity and Pressure

For several weeks, Ariel complained regularly about work. The usual: boss, colleagues, everyone putting pressure on him. I eventually homed in on the fact that Ariel's most frequent complaint was that he had too much to do. I then uttered the relevant cliché:

Th: No one can do more than one thing at a time, so what's on the to-do list doesn't really matter.
Cl: It matters to them.
Th: You mean the company?
Cl: Yes. Them.
Th: So? Could you do more than you are doing if they pushed you harder?
Cl: No.
Th: So what's the point of fretting?
Cl: [excitedly] Wow, I just realized what it is! I think I created an identity that involves being able to do everything on the list. So I *have* to do everything. I wouldn't be me if I didn't.
Th: So the pressure is really coming from you. It's you who creates the pressure and therefore the anxiety.
Cl: I think so now. My identity makes it impossible for me to feel good without having completed all that crap. It's crazy.

80   *A Little More on Anxiety*

Ariel's identity had locked him into the situation that was causing him distress. There were certainly demands on him at work, but the bulk of the anxiety he was feeling derived from his own mind.

* * *

In the next chapter, we'll look at self-evaluation and its effect on relationships.

9 Self-Evaluation and Relationships

"All the world's a stage," wrote Shakespeare in "As You Like It." A stage, indeed, on which people project what they believe themselves to be, or what they would like to believe themselves to be, in hope that they will be able to believe it if they can persuade others to believe it. The script, in other words, is written by self-evaluation.

Self-evaluation can play havoc with social relationships. It tends to create expectations that are either unrealistic or self-defeating. People who value themselves too highly may turn down good potential partners. They may also mistreat those who love them. People who undervalue themselves may not go after what is possible. They may also get exploited, perchance by people who value themselves too highly.

Self-evaluation also confuses the task of evaluating others. People who base their assessments of others on their own self-evaluation are likely to make serious mistakes. To survive and prosper in the market system, or anywhere else, for that matter, one needs to make reality-based assessments of other people.

There is, of course, a counter argument. One often hears that a realistic appraisal of oneself is the best way to arrive at an accurate assessment of other. But I don't think so. As Robert Burns put it, rare is the fellow with the gift "to see ourselves as others see us."

On the Opinion of Others

So many people worry about the opinion of others! There is, of course, an evolutionary basis for this concern: survival. Our species descends from a long line of group-living monkeys and apes who had to keep an eye out for the other members of the group. In the early days of our own species, when we too lived in small groups, everyone was in fact interdependent. Individuals who didn't behave in a way that was acceptable to other band members risked being ostracized, a fate equivalent to death. As a result, everyone was obliged to worry about what other people thought.

82 *Self-Evaluation and Relationships*

Obviously the situation is not the same today. We can survive as loners, iconoclasts, and rebels. Although we do have to pay attention to the opinions of certain people, including bosses, colleagues, and family members, we are largely free to do our own thing. Nevertheless, people now worry about what total strangers might think, even when no adverse effect is possible. And they often worry about the most trivial matters—how their hair looks or what kind of clothes they're wearing or whether they said the wrong thing at a party.

As many social critics have pointed out, advertising, that ill-begotten offspring of the market system, feeds off these types of concern and magnifies them. We denizens of the market constantly encounter evaluations by some people of other people—in the news, in sports, in movies, on TV shows. And those judgments are accepted as natural and inevitable. In effect, many people now imagine that they have to reach into the minds of others, to make sure that the opinions others have of them are positive, or at least acceptable.

To a significant degree, this worry is connected to opinion of self. The opinions of others—even insignificant others—become emotionally fraught primarily because they affect one's opinion of self. If a criticism by an acquaintance or a funny look by a stranger can produce pain and suffering, it's because that opinion, and that look, lower our opinion of self. It follows, as we proposed in Chapter 5, that if we don't have an opinion of self, the opinions of those who are not important to us will lose their ability to swamp us with emotion.

Clients often then argue: "But others do judge me . . ."

In responding, several important distinctions have to be made. The therapist has to first dispose of the *boss issue*; it's in our own self-interest to care about the opinions of those who have power over us. Like Russ, who had to learn how to avoid threatening or annoying his boss and colleagues (see Chapter 4), everyone in a hierarchical organization must recognize the people in power.

Then there is the issue of family and friends. Obviously, it is both natural and desirable to take what they think into account, both because of our affection for them and because if they are happy, we're likely to be happier. The therapist has to be able to make a distinction between excessive concern and real caring.

It sometimes helps to go over the distinction between *behavior* and *emotional reaction*. It's often in an individual's interest to behave in ways that take the opinions of others, even insignificant others, into account. But it is rarely, if ever, useful to suffer an overpowering emotional reaction to disapproval or criticism. Interacting with others is far easier and more pleasurable when one isn't worrying about what they think.

Please note: The following extracts from case notes are designed to show the connection between self-evaluation and couples issues. These passages do not pretend to provide an overview of couples therapy.

The Dugans

Mrs. Dugan was extremely sensitive to what her husband said and thought about her. So they fought about it. A lot.

Mr. Dugan was a drinker. She was the long-suffering wife. The week before the session he had wanted her to go to his brother's house to help with a party. She happened to know that his brother didn't need help and said so. He responded by accusing her of hating his family. She was devastated by this comment and had been trying to prove him wrong ever since.

At her individual session, she was visibly upset. I asked her why she cared about his opinion of her relationship with his family:

Cl: Of course I care. He's my husband.
Th: Sure, but it's just his opinion. Do you have to react?
Cl: I don't see how I could just ignore it.
Th: Often enough, people only care about the opinion of others if they have a bad opinion of themselves.
Cl: [excited] Oh, I've got a lot of that. I always think I'm not good enough.
Th: Really. What are you not good enough at?
Cl: Not smart enough. Not helpful enough. Not generous enough. My appearance. It never stops.
Th: Really? [She was quite beautiful and clearly intelligent.] How long have you had those thoughts about yourself?
Cl: Forever.
Th: Which "not good enough" is the most punishing?
Cl: I'm not a doctor.
Th: So?
Cl: My parents wanted a doctor. They always wanted me to do better in school, to get ahead, make money. Like other kids in the family. They always pointed out how great the others were doing . . .

From there, we eventually went to the remedy.

Th: You probably won't be able to solve the problem by trying to think that you ARE good enough. You aren't.
Cl: [shocked look] What do you mean?
Th: There is no such quantity as "good enough." It's an imaginary concept. No actual level of achievement is either "good enough" or "not good enough." Do you understand now what I meant?

84 *Self-Evaluation and Relationships*

Cl: I think so.

Th: Good. You were worried there for a minute.

Cl: It was a shock.

Th: The only way out is to stop having an opinion—stop judging yourself. You are not "good enough" and not "not good enough."

Cl: I would love that, but how can I stop what I'm thinking?

Th: Well, that's not easy. It takes work, but that's what we're going to do.

Cl: Well, but what's that got to do with his slander?

Th: Maybe you could just let him think what he thinks?

We then went to catch and dismiss and began the work.

Clients are often concerned about the opinions of others because they are looking for "acceptance." But, as we pointed out in Chapter 4, acceptance is not a physical emanation from other people. Rather, it's an internal state, one that starts with self-acceptance. If you accept yourself, you're not as vulnerable to the slings and arrows of in-groups and cliques. If you accept yourself, you are good enough.

Self-Sacrifice and Opinion of Self

It's a fact. Some people turn themselves into martyrs. Many explanations exist and many causes too. Maintaining an opinion of self is one of them.

Pamela

Pamela, a highly successful, workaholic upper-level manager, was also the matriarch of a demanding family. She felt compelled to meet all their demands, without reservation. As her children grew, they demanded more time and attention; as her husband got older, so did he. By the time she came in to (individual) therapy, she was exhausted.

While some of the demands on her seemed reasonable, a number of them didn't. To take just one example, her husband wanted her to join him on regular visits to his aging, domineering mother; he didn't get along with his mother and wanted his wife along to make conversation. Pamela made no corresponding demands on him, no apparent *quid pro quo.*

Why did she attempt to satisfy endless demands like these? The answer came slowly. Each and every demand, it seemed, provoked the same question: "Am I a good-enough person if I don't do it?" If the answer she gave herself was "not good enough," she would accede to the demand. She had never, apparently, asked herself if a request was fair or reasonable.

At first Pamela dismissed my attempts to raise those kinds of questions. We had to start by exploring the origins of this rather awful compulsion.

Self-Evaluation and Relationships   85

What we found was rebellion against the values of the market system! Pamela grew up in a culture that emphasized community. She was horrified by American individualism. She was doing what she was doing in order to conform to the quality of a good person in her society of origin.

I had a tricky problem: how to diminish her willingness to be exploited without making her feel like a bad person. The solution lay in reemphasizing reciprocity (reciprocal altruism), a subject which is treated at length in *Exiles From Eden: Psychotherapy From an Evolutionary Perspective* (1989). The basic idea there is simple: Willingness to help is a survival mechanism designed to create a web of supportive relationships. If others are not reciprocating, it's natural to limit one's own helping behavior (see Chapter 2).

Pamela got the idea fairly quickly and discovered that she didn't have to sacrifice herself in order to maintain her opinion of herself and keep the affection of her family.

Assessing Mate Value

When self-evaluation is used to assess one's value as a mate, the results can be somewhat strange.

Hal

Hal had a once-in-a-lifetime sexual relationship with Heather. Their lovemaking transcended what he himself thought he was capable of experiencing. But he kept finding fault with her. In session, he would often mutter something about not believing they would end up together:

Th: Why that prediction?
Cl: I don't know. It just seems that way.
Th: Does she put you down?
Cl: [excitedly] No, that's it! She looks up to me. She worships me. I find it uncomfortable.
Th: Explain that to me.
Cl: I'm not sure I can explain it to myself.
Th: Try.
Cl: I think it makes me feel like a fraud. I know I'm not what she thinks I am. I'm not nearly that special. It freezes me up.

It took a while to make sense of what seemed like a strange complaint but eventually we figured it out. Hal constantly rated himself and found himself wanting. He was so conscious of his faults, and so put-off by them, that he

86   *Self-Evaluation and Relationships*

experienced her admiration as a flaw in her—a lack of perceptiveness, an unacceptable naiveté. As a result, she didn't seem like a viable partner. He had, in fact, been much more comfortable with her rigid, moralistic, and harshly critical predecessor—the woman who had hauled him off to therapy. Once Hal understood that the problem was his view of himself, he was better able to accept Heather's admiration.

Self-Evaluation and Criticism

Some spouses criticize, quibble, carp, nitpick, and sneer. It can be very hard to stop them. Look for self-criticism; it's a good bet.

Jack and Jill

Jack and Jill believed that criticism was part of the fabric of relationships, an inherent and essential part of being together. Neither one could imagine interacting with the other without pointing out flaws. It seemed outrageous to both of them to think that they could ever relate to each other differently: "How else will we tell each other what's wrong?"

I tried for several weeks to bring about a change, but nothing helped. Finally, I understood: They were both *self*-critical. They hated themselves. Not only that. They both believed that self-criticism was necessary in order to "improve" and to get ahead. In other words, they were using self-criticism as motivation (see Chapter 7). Criticism of the other, then, made perfect sense: Improve oneself, improve one's spouse.

Neither of them had an identity that was independent of their level of success and achievement. Neither found identity in belonging (to one another). Neither was content with self, so neither could be content with the other.

Clearly, self-acceptance had to precede success with couples therapy. Each needed to experience a corrective environment and to acquire what might be called the anti-self-criticism tool-kit. Accordingly, I suggested that they come separately.

I began by working on it with Jack. Here's an extract from his therapy:

Th: So when she continues to criticize you, you feel hurt and you retaliate.
Cl: Yes. It feels like what I felt when my father criticized me. What we talked about last time.
Th: I remember. So the criticism is triggering traumatic memories. Have you at all been able to catch it as it happens?
Cl: Occasionally. Usually it still escapes me.
Th: Sure. It takes time. Let's go back to the feeling. Can you identify anything you're thinking at the moment?

Self-Evaluation and Relationships **87**

Cl: No, not really. I just don't feel I'm good enough.

Th: Good enough for who?

Cl: For anyone.

Th: That's a horrible feeling.

Cl: No kidding.

Th: But wait a minute. Is that a feeling or a thought?

Cl: A thought, I guess.

Th: You're right, a thought.

Cl: So it's what I'm thinking that's hurting?

Th: Yes, I think it's a double whammy, the traumatic memories plus the awful thought that you're not good enough. Almost surely a very old thought. A conclusion you reached because of your father's criticism.

Cl: What can I do?

Th: Eventually you'll need to accept yourself as a flawed person. Perhaps it would help if you circle back to the idea of being a male mammal. Something that can't be judged, that doesn't depend on performance to be OK.

Cl: I go there often but I can't stay there in the face of her criticism.

Th: It will come.

It took time but once Jack understood that blaming someone for his pain was not productive, he was in a position to restart couples therapy.

John and Johanna

John and Johanna also lived to make points with each other. Early on in their relationship they had somewhat enjoyed the sparring. Now they were constantly annoyed with each other. Sex was a distant memory.

They both had good jobs but that meant that they spent their workdays competing. More or less without realizing it, they had begun to treat each other the way they themselves were treated in the rat race. They both had to be on guard against threats to their self-esteem. They both had to maintain their image of themselves. They had learned to treat other people as potentially hostile competitors:

Th: Let me understand. If you don't win in one of these exchanges, you are defeated. You lose.

Cl: Of course. And losing feels terrible.

Th: Of course.

Cl: No?

Th: What if I were to tell you that the prime rule in a relationship is "If you do win, you lose."

88   *Self-Evaluation and Relationships*

Cl: How is that possible?

Th: Well, if you defeat your spouse, your spouse will be unhappy. You'll then have an unhappy spouse who will probably try to make you unhappy.

Cl: I never really thought about that.

Progress was difficult because they were deeply mired in the trench warfare that had infiltrated their relationship. Active listening (Gordon, 1977) helped because it interfered with the reflexive counterattacks. I also repeatedly modeled non-agonistic responses. Eventually they started, tentatively, to try them out.

Self-Evaluation, Power, and Sex

Jerry and Janice

Jerry knew, from friends and elsewhere, that women sometimes experience men's desire for intercourse as coming "out of the blue." He wanted to avoid that pitfall. He wanted above all to believe that unlike so many men, he was in the thoughtful-lover category—a sensitive, new-age guy, as Christine Lavin described in a song by that name.

As a lover, Jerry liked to play. At odd moments in the day or evening, he would come up behind Janice, caress her, kiss her on the neck, and generally fool around. He made it a point of pride to initiate intercourse only when she was responsive. He believed that his frequent playful approaches were keeping him in the good-guy category.

For a number of years, Janice had responded in kind. But then something changed. She stopped responding positively. She began to interpret his approach to her as his way of exerting power over her. Over time, she got angrier and angrier. Eventually she laid down the law: "From now on, you can only approach me for sex when I give you permission in advance." Sex had morphed into power.

Jerry was surprised and then hurt. He was not conscious of any power-related intentions. His first response was to stop approaching her at all. After a while, though, he tried following her rules. "At first, I felt like a servant. After a while, it made me feel like a eunuch."

Eventually, we realized that the change had occurred sometime after Janice received a big promotion. In her new position, she had significantly more authority and responsibility. At home, she was often preoccupied by matters at work. She frequently reported that she believed she had to outdo the men. Jerry's notion, that he could approach her, however playfully, whenever he wanted, no longer fit with her view of herself.

Self-Evaluation and Relationships **89**

Therapy was not able to reconcile their two views. The marriage slid into divorce.

Arguing and the Opinion of Self

Many "discussions" are really attempts by one spouse to change the opinion of the other. Here's a typical example:

Her: You really wanted to hurt me.
Him: No I didn't. I just thought your cousin was right.
Her: You never take my side.
Him: I just try to be fair.
Her: You always deny that you try to hurt me.
Him: You just imagine that. You never look at the facts.

Defense against attributions, in support of one's opinion of self, explains why so much arguing about apparent trivialities can get so intense. If you can let your spouse think what he or she wants about you, you won't need to argue.

Charlie

Charlie argued almost permanently with his wife:

Th: Tell me why you keep doing that?
Cl: I have to. What she says shakes me.
Th: Do you know what exactly you feel?
Cl: Anxious. Fear. I don't know.
Th: What are you afraid of?
Cl: My own feelings.
Th: Really! Tell me about that. What does she say that causes you fear?
Cl: What she thinks affects how I see myself. I'm not where I'm supposed to be in life. She makes me see myself as a failure.

I then sought to shift Charlie's concept of who and what he was, using the approaches described earlier. Charlie was eventually able to see himself as a creature and to identify a set of traits that could not be evaluated. Therapy then focused on the conclusion to be drawn from this insight:

Th: So you can see that what other people think can't have any effect on this part of your self-concept or identity. You're undeniably a male mammal, whatever else someone thinks of you. So, if your wife says

90   *Self-Evaluation and Relationships*

something that causes you pain, you have to catch what's happening, remember your new self-definition, and shift your attention to the sensations in your body. Then you will be able to respond in a way that will help rather than harm your marriage.

That, of course, is a tall order and takes work, the kind of work that therapists normally do to integrate an insight and make it useful. Charlie got the hang of it fairly quickly, but that is unusual. There is no set timetable for success.

***

The next chapter contains additional dialogs illustrating and expanding on themes developed in this book.

10 Illustrations from the Files

This chapter contains additional dialogs showing how quickly a therapist who is on the alert for hints of self-evaluation can initiate productive interventions. The dialogs expand on and illustrate the themes and principles laid out in previous chapters.

Although clients come to therapy with what seem to be very different problems and issues, much of what is bothering them is generated or exacerbated by the dark side of the market system—comparison and excess competitiveness. Attention to this dimension of a client's problems can often provide immediate relief while leading to a discussion of older, deeper levels.

Sometimes a client's self-evaluation is embedded in a matrix of self-defeating ideas and emotions, but sometimes it seems to have had a virgin birth—no antecedent from childhood, no mental illness. In such cases, the influence of the market system in promoting self-evaluation is most clear and easiest to reverse. "Roberta" is one of those relatively uncomplicated cases.

Roberta: From "Worrying About What People Think" to Opinion of Self

After Roberta had done some good work about her drinking, she asked if she needed to continue to come. I said it was up to her, and asked if there was anything that she was worried about. She immediately offered that she worries too much about what other people think.

Th: Why?

Cl: I feel terrible if I think someone has a bad opinion of me. Just yesterday, my mom asked me if I had finished my assignment. I told her I had gotten through half of it. I spent the rest of the week thinking about what she thought of that. My stomach was in knots, I had a horrible sinking feeling in my chest.

Th: Do you know why you had that reaction?

92   *Illustrations from the Files*

Cl: No. Do you?

Th: I might have a clue.

Cl: [laughing] Really. Tell me.

Th: I could but it's better if you figure it out for yourself.

Cl: Now I don't have a clue.

Th: Think. What happens in your head when your body is being wracked like that.

Cl: I keep thinking about what she said.

Th: Right, but is there anything else?

Cl: Do you mean my thoughts about me?

Th: Yes. What thoughts?

Cl: Am I a good person or not. I think about that all the time.

Th: Why do you do that?

Cl: Doesn't everyone want to be a good person?

Th: Perhaps, but do you have to think about it all the time?

Cl: I never thought about that.

Th: Besides, why do you have an opinion at all?

Cl: An opinion about me?

Th: Yes.

Cl: Doesn't everybody?

Th: No.

Cl: Really?

Th: OK, let's see what we can find. When you think someone has a bad opinion of you, your own opinion changes, right?

Cl: Right. Yes. You mean I don't have to do that?

Th: No, you don't.

Cl: You're kidding.

Th: No. But it isn't easy to change it.

From there, we went to recognize and dismiss. Almost immediately, Roberta become excited and enthusiastic about the process:

Cl: So each time is an opportunity to practice!

Th: Fantastic. Usually I have to explain to people that it's an opportunity and here you've got it already.

At the next session, I brought up one more point:

Th: I think you can now see that for the most part, when you were worrying about what people think, you were actually managing your *own* emotions. It wasn't about them, it was about you.

Cl: Nasty. What a waste of time.

Illustrations from the Files   93

Roberta wasn't attached to her concern for the opinions of others. Within a few sessions, she was able to catch herself doing it and move on, a result that has to be considered exceptional. But relatively quick results with the intervention are not uncommon, presumably because it drives to the heart of thoughts, emotions, and identity.

Bobo: From "Lack of Confidence" to Opinion of Self

Bobo, a rather unassertive new client, offered that he lacked "confidence."

Th: I doubt if confidence is the right term for what you are experiencing. It doesn't lead to any particular action.
Cl: What would be better?
Th: Let's wait on that. You've told me that sometimes you are brimming with confidence and sometimes you're not. When you're not, how do you see yourself? Do you have a high opinion of yourself?
Cl: Of course not. I think I'm really terrible.
Th: But at other times, your opinion is different, right? You think you're actually very competent.
Cl: Right.
Th: Why do you have an opinion?

Here it became necessary to deal with the usual shock and incomprehension. Then we proceeded as described next (in a passage reproduced in an earlier chapter):

Th: How do you *feel* when you *think* you're terrific?
Cl: On top of the world, of course.
Th: Can you describe what you actually feel, in your body?
Cl: [long hesitation] Erect. Expansive. Really aware of surroundings.
Th: Energized?
Cl: Yes. Exactly!
Th: And when your opinion is low?
Cl: Bent over. Tired. Like I'm being tied up.
Th: Constricted?
Cl: Exactly.
Th: Now you can see why you seek approval. It shifts your opinion and that changes the way you feel. It's like dope. In a sense you're addicted.

Eventually Bobo wanted to know how not having an opinion would affect his interactions with others. He was worried that it would compromise his ability to empathize, which he considered a strong suit:

94 *Illustrations from the Files*

Th: Well, it seems to me, you would be thinking about the issue, or the other guy, not about yourself. You wouldn't be worried because your view of yourself wouldn't be at stake.

Cl: Do you think I've been using other people to make myself feel good?

Th: Not deliberately, of course.

Cl: That's awful.

Th: Not really. You weren't doing any harm. But there are better ways.

Grant: From "Fear of Speaking Out" to Opinion of Self

Grant started by telling me about a recent incident at work. He had spoken up during a meeting to say that he didn't think a proposed plan would work:

Cl: I immediately began to worry that I was out of line. I went to my boss right after the meeting. He didn't seem concerned.

Th: So he wasn't concerned?

Cl: Not very much. But it shook me because I constantly monitor the situation at work. I have to measure myself against all the others.

Th: You do? Why?

Cl: [hesitation] I feel better if I think that I'm better than everyone. I have to think that I'm the best.

Th: What happens if you don't think you're the best?

Cl: I don't feel good. I get confused. I lose track of conversations.

Th: Do you think the other people all recognize that you're the best?

Cl: Probably not.

Th: Do you think they all have to think that they're the best?

Cl: I never thought about it.

Th: So your opinion may well be different from all the other people in the firm.

Cl: Hmn. I suppose so. I never really thought about it.

Th: Why do you have an opinion?

Cl: I guess I never thought about it. It's an interesting question . . .

Grant's fear of speaking out was the product of his need to make sure that he was liked and respected by everyone. His freedom of action was constrained by his need to manage his opinion of self, which forced him to try to manage the opinions of others. Grant had a hard time recognizing this procedure so it took him several weeks to begin to overcome it.

Christian: From "Conflict" to Opinion of Self

Th: So what's going on at work? You getting that website done?

Cl: It's slow. I'm fighting with the engineer, and I really don't like conflict

Th: Really. Why?

Illustrations from the Files 95

Cl: It makes me feel bad.
Th: What are you feeling?
Cl: I get knots in my stomach.
Th: Do any thoughts go along with that?
Cl: I suppose so. I start asking myself if it's my fault.
Th: Then what?
Cl: I start questioning my ability.

This jump to negative self-analysis is somewhat unusual for its speed and lack of intermediate stages, but it highlights the essentials.

Christian's dislike of conflict was traceable to dimly remembered events in his upbringing. Once he brought them up into consciousness, he was able to successfully implement the tools I had given him.

Billy: From "Anxiety" to Opinion of Self[1]

Relaxation and meditation had not helped Billy, a fairly prominent engineer, to reduce his ongoing anxiety. Where to go next was the question in my mind, and I didn't have an answer. Then I remembered that in previous sessions, there were hints that he had doubts about his own abilities:

Th: I was wondering about something. You've been pretty successful. Do you run any doubts about your competence?
Cl: Sure, doesn't everybody?
Th: Can you tell me about them?
Cl: It's pretty normal. Whenever I come across someone who makes more money than me, or just someone who has achieved a lot, I ask myself: "Why don't I have that or why didn't I do that?"
Th: Really.
Cl: Yeah, I always compare myself to someone who is above me, never below. I don't know why I do that.
Th: So you must always feel pressure to do better.
Cl: Yes. Of course.
Th: Well then, you must always be trying to form an opinion of yourself.
Cl: Isn't everybody?
Th: Does that matter?
Cl: I guess not, after all. This is about me.
Th: So why do you have an opinion at all?
Cl: That's a weird question.
Th: Really? What good is your opinion of you?

Here we went into the usual discussion of the irrelevancy of self-evaluation.

96 *Illustrations from the Files*

At a subsequent session we went after another anxiety-provoking procedure:

Th: My guess is, you're always thinking about outcomes.

Cl: Yes, of course. Doesn't everybody?

Th: Well, that could well be the reason for the anxiety. That's a way of thinking. If you focus on outcomes, nothing stops you from imagining a negative outcome, and bingo, you're afraid.

Cl: I do that. All the time.

Th: OK. But how to stop? I'm going to introduce a distinction that might make stopping easier. There's a difference between thinking about decisions and thinking about outcomes.

Cl: Yes. I can see it. If I can do something about the outcome, it's worth thinking about. But only then.

Th: Right.

From there, we went to recognize and dismiss and continued as usual.

Timothy: From "Fear of Not Getting Approval" to Opinion of Self

Th: Tell me why you're upset at your boss.

Cl: She just never says anything.

Th: Did she say you did anything wrong?

Cl: No.

Th: No bad reviews?

Cl: No. But she doesn't show any appreciation, no recognition for what I do.

Th: So there is no indication that she has a problem with you.

Cl: Are you telling me I'm imagining things?

Th: No, certainly not. I have no reason to disbelieve you. But perhaps she is just a bad manager?

Cl: The rest of them are the same. Do the same.

Th: So what happens to you during the day?

Cl: I get down on myself, that's all.

Th: Your opinion of yourself goes down?

Cl: I suppose you could call it that.

Th: So unless you get strokes from folks your self-evaluation goes down?

Cl: Right. Isn't that normal?

Th: Well tell me. Why do you have an opinion about yourself?

Cl: Come on, everybody does.

Th: And it's your opinion that changes.

Cl: I guess so.

Th: Then what happens?

Illustrations from the Files 97

Cl: I start to beat myself up, of course.

Th: So you're doing it to yourself.

Cl: I suppose. What am I supposed to do?

Th: Well, that's what we're going to see now. But clearly if you weren't beating yourself up, you wouldn't be so distressed, would you?

We eventually realized that Timothy had determined that he was not really good at one of the skills needed to succeed in that office:

Cl: What am I supposed to do, pretend to myself that I'm good at it?

Th: There's a difference between not being good at a skill and not being a good-enough person. Or even a good-enough employee.

Cl: What is it? I don't know it.

Th: Well look, there are hundreds of things I'm not good at. Does that make me a not-good-enough person?

Cl: I suppose not. No, of course not.

Th: Right. Not being good enough at something in particular doesn't require us to make a global assessment of self.

Cl: I get it. But how to keep remembering it?

Th: First make the connection to your feelings. When you aren't making that distinction, you become worthless in your own eyes.

Cl: That's true.

Th: Which feels terrible, right?

Cl: You got it.

Th: So maybe when you feel that bad feeling, it can remind you to catch what you're doing and make the distinction.

It took Timothy a few sessions to make the distinction clear enough to catch the negative thoughts. Once he did, he was able to go to work if not with joy, at least without misery.

Dwight: From "Worrying About Money" to Opinion of Self[2]

Dwight offered that most of his anxiety swirled around money:

Cl: The pregnancy is costing a lot more than I thought it would. Insurance doesn't pay for all kinds of things. There's expenses with the baby coming on, Christmas presents for the family. And my car just died. We're trying to save for retirement too. It feels overwhelming.

Th: Yeah, you look distressed.

98   *Illustrations from the Files*

Cl: We're so focused on the negative. I wish there was something positive to work on.

Th: What would that be like?

Cl: [struggling with tears] Don't know. I'm not happy and I should be. I have a job, a wife that I love, a baby on the way, money in the bank, but I don't feel happy.

Th: Tell me, when you think about the money problems, do you have any thoughts about yourself?

Cl: That I can't get it together. I can't handle it. I'm no good.

Th: You have a comfortable life, but you don't think you made it happen. It was luck and it might run out?

Cl: Yeah.

Th: And it's only money that brings on this thought?

Cl: Well, money and I guess everything to do with it. My getting it.

Th: So if you think about your situation, everything is OK, but if you think about you and your role in it, you fall apart.

Cl: I guess so. Yes, that seems to be it.

Th: So why do you think about you and your role?

Cl: What do you mean? I always have. How can you not?

Th: What if you could [not think about it]?

Cl: That would be great, I suppose.

Th: What I want you to try is, every time the thought that you can't handle it comes to your mind, you catch it and label it. Just say "there it is again." Don't try to refute it or argue with it. Just label it . . .

It took a couple of weeks for Dwight to get the hang of it. During that time, we explored some messages he got from his parents in early life about money. Recognizing those messages made labeling his negative thoughts easier. He soon stopped agonizing about his abilities and was able to focus his energies on other aspects of his life.

Greg: From "Too Much Leisure" to Opinion of Self

On Monday, Greg's day off, he found that while he was completely free and didn't have to do anything in particular, he didn't feel free:

Cl: It made me anxious.

Th: Why?

Cl: I had to decide which I *should* do.

Th: Should?

Cl: Yes. I had to decide between doing something frivolous, like a movie with my wife, or working on my project.

Illustrations from the Files 99

Th: What did you *want* to do?

Cl: It's tangled. I wanted to work on my project, but I also wanted to just do something frivolous.

Th: Was anything at stake?

Cl: Well, it's my identity.

Th: How's that?

Cl: Well, sometimes I think that I always decide for the frivolous, so it would confirm that opinion of me.

Th: Which would mean what?

Cl: That I'm no good.

We discussed this for some time before he began challenging his self-condemnation. Then:

Cl: I really have a hard time separating wanting something fun and thinking that I *should* do something. That also feels like wanting.

Th: Really? How can that be?

Cl: It goes back to my parents. My father got into the sports industry because he liked playing tennis, but his job was not in sports, it was managing a facility. My mother also just did what she had to. There was nothing creative about it.

Th: So you don't *want* to be like your parents and that feels like a want, to you.

Cl: Right.

Th: OK then. We have to figure out how to make your real wants more salient.

The following week went well until the weekend.

Cl: For a while I was looking at things differently. I could pay attention to what I wanted. I could see the difference between what I had to do and what I wanted to do. Mostly I was calm. But when the weekend came, it changed.

Th: What happened?

Cl: I started a to-do list and my wife had a few items, and then I got overwhelmed. I couldn't prioritize.

We went looking for the reason. What emerged was a connection between completing tasks and having worth. The connection was embedded in a related set of beliefs, namely that his friends and family only valued him and only wanted to spend time with him because of the deeds he accomplished. "Why would they want to be around me if I didn't have worth?" This taught

100 *Illustrations from the Files*

us that he was still struggling with opinion of self. It took several more sessions to undo his belief in self-evaluation.

Th: Do you think there is a box, an "I-have-worth box" that you can get into? An objective determination?
Cl: I don't know. It feels like it.
Th: Right. But the only thing you can change with this procedure is your own opinion about your worth.
Cl: And I'm not supposed to have an opinion. I know. But it keeps cropping up. I get the idea at times but then I lose it.
Th: Well, we'll just have to keep chasing your opinion around.

Derek: From "Too Many Demands" to Opinion of Self

Derek said his job was exhausting him:

Th: What's going on there?
Cl: There are too many demands on my time.
Th: People asking for your help?
Cl: Yes.
Th: So you're helping people?
Cl: Yeah, I get a kick out of that, but it doesn't leave me time to get to what I need to do.
Th: Has your boss told you to do something else?
Cl: No, he says I'm doing what I'm supposed to do.
Th: Tell me, do you take any pride in being so much in demand?
Cl: Not really.
Th: Why not?
Cl: I try to please people, but I haven't been able to please everyone.
Th: Why do you try?
Cl: I don't want anyone to have a bad opinion of me.

Derek had to understand that his goal was unreasonable before he could start dismissing the thought. It took some weeks and a good deal of discussion.

Priscilla: From "The Sight of Another Woman" to Opinion of Self

Priscilla, who happened to be a very beautiful woman, frequently got upset when her fiancée commented on another woman, usually a TV actress. They often quarreled about it.

Illustrations from the Files 101

Th: Does he express desire for them or make inappropriate remarks?

Cl: Not really. All he has to do is say anything about how she looks, or even about her acting. I have a fit.

Th: What does a fit mean? What actually happens in you when he does that?

Cl: My first thought is always "He doesn't react that way to *my* body." Then there's a whole cascade: "Maybe my body doesn't please him." "Maybe I'm not enough for him." From there it can go to "Maybe I'll never be able to please anyone for long."

Th: Have you always had thoughts like this?

Cl: Yes, as long as I can remember.

Th: What do you do when that is happening?

Cl: I fight it. I tell myself that I'm very attractive. I remind myself that other people tell me I'm attractive, but usually that doesn't help until it's too late. By then I've been miserable and we've had a fight.

Priscilla's opinion of self was controlling her relationship and probably always had. Her two techniques—arguing and making affirmations—were useless. She had to find a way to stay away from thoughts about herself. Therapy took the usual direction: recognize, label and dismiss, focus on the feelings, etc.

Boris: From "Not Having Something to Say" to Opinion of Self

Boris came in to his session talking about his day and looking distracted:

Th: I have the impression that you have something else on your mind.

Cl: No, it's not that. I don't have anything in particular to talk about.

Th: How does that make you feel?

Cl: I'm feeling like a failure.

Th: Feeling like a failure. That's a thought, really. How do you *feel* when you think that thought?

Cl: Terrible. Hopeless. I wonder if it's worthwhile going on.

Th: So why do you keep on thinking thoughts that make you feel bad?

Cl: Aren't they valuable? Isn't that how we make ourselves better?

Th: So you think you aren't good enough?

Cl: I never think I'm good enough. I'm afraid that if I thought that for a minute, I would lose my place in the world. My job, everything . . .

Th: Not good enough. Would you agree with me that the phrase expresses an opinion?

Cl: [as so often happens] Well, it's my opinion but it's true.

102 *Illustrations from the Files*

Th: Why do you have an opinion?

Cl: What do you mean?

Here once again it became necessary to deal with the usual surprise and incomprehension before moving on:

Th: It looks like you think you have to keep running just to stay in the same place.

Cl: Yeah. That's the way it seems.

Th: How long have you had that sense?

Cl: I think it goes back to childhood. The only thing my father ever talked about was getting ahead. Grades was all he cared about. I had to be the best, get into the best college, so I could make money. Otherwise I'd be a loser.

The rest of therapy was devoted to uprooting that idea. It didn't come easy. Boris was attached to the idea and feared giving it up. He needed lots of reassurance and many low-risk opportunities to act differently.

Isaiah: From "Inability to Delegate" to Opinion of Self

Isaiah had an internally consistent web of ideas that was driving him mercilessly. He had to work day and night in order to stay ahead of the imaginary posse that was always after him.

Th: Can't you delegate?

Cl: You don't understand. I can't just turn any of the work over to someone else.

Th: Why not?

Cl: I could still be blamed.

Th: Being blamed is the first thing that comes to mind?

Cl: Yeah, it is. I can't get away from it.

Th: Even if someone else was responsible?

Cl: You're damn right. Besides, if someone else knew anything about what is going on, he could find out about me.

Th: Find out what?

Cl: That I'm a fraud.

Th: Really, a fraud. What makes you think that?

Cl: Look, my success is due to luck, that's all. I could be found out any time.

We went to work on dismantling the structure but found some serious resistance . . .

Illustrations from the Files 103

Cl: Look, the only time I have ever felt useful is when I'm working. If I wasn't working all the time, I would be prone to thinking more poorly of myself and that's not fun.

"Fraud" and "luck," those mass-produced instruments of self-torture, were the keys to this structure. It took some time to dismantle it. Isaiah had to realize that the procedure he was using—self-evaluation—was unable to produce a realistic self-definition or a useful understanding of the world.

Bart: From "Conversing Without Breaks" to Opinion of Self

Bart was an executive in a creative position:

Th: I noticed that you don't leave any breaks in your conversation, no space for the other person to join in.
Cl: Yeah, well, I've always thought of myself as uninteresting. I can't imagine that anyone would be interested in me. So I try to compensate. I keep interjecting new things into the conversation. That way I can keep it interesting.
Th: That's a very negative opinion about yourself.
Cl: Yeah, I guess so.
Th: Why do you have an opinion? [and on from there]

A Follow-Up Example

Eric had been working on his opinion of self for a few weeks when this dialog happened.

Cl: When I make a mistake, it affects me. I feel it. But when I do something positive, competent, it has no effect unless someone else notices it. What does this mean?
Th: I think it might have to do with grandiosity.
Cl: Grandiosity?
Th: I think so. Consider this. If you do something competently, well, you think you're supposed to. It goes without saying. You already knew you were perfect, competent, exceptional. So nothing changes. But if it's something negative, well, that changes everything. It means you aren't what you thought you were. On the other hand, if someone else notices, that's proof that you were right after all, so you get a boost.
Cl: Well, that makes sense anyway. It's logical.

104 *Illustrations from the Files*

At the end of the session, I reminded him:

Th: Just remember, you aren't good or bad, competent or not, you just are.

Cl: [after a few seconds] Wow, I caught it. Just as you said "I wasn't good, I just was," I felt the onslaught of the wind of negativity. I never caught it so early before. It's always at the gates, isn't it?

The opportunity to use the "opinion of self" intervention provides a unique short-cut to self-definition, emotion, and identity. It isn't always appropriate, but it can be a useful addition to a therapist's armamentarium.

A Final Word

I would like to conclude this book with a bit of self-disclosure that worked out well.

A client who was struggling challenged me:

Cl: Come on, don't you rate yourself?

Th: Sure, I catch myself doing it every once and a while. When I was young, I did it more often. But I worked at it. Now I have distance on those thoughts. I can even have the thought that I am the worst therapist in the world. The thought doesn't bother me now. It doesn't affect my mood and I don't take it seriously.

Cl: [shocked] But then you must have terribly low self-esteem!

Th: Do you think so? Not really. At other times, I think a different thought about myself. I catch myself thinking I'm great. It doesn't excite me now. I'm aware that my *self*-evaluation doesn't make any difference to anyone and isn't objective. So what difference does it make what my opinion is? You have your evaluation of me, everybody I see has theirs. Some will be high, some will be low. It is what it is.

Cl: [after some hesitation] I think I see. Some people think I'm ugly, some people think I'm attractive. I should just hang out with the ones who think I'm attractive.

You are who you are. So is everyone else. No more, no less. Self-acceptance is the only reliable remedy for recurring thoughts about the self.

Notes

1. Ten lines of this dialogue were used in the Introduction.
2. Fourteen lines of this dialogue were used in the Introduction.

References

Balikci, Asen. 1970. *The Netsilik Eskimo*. Garden City, NY: Natural History Press.

Benson, Herbert. 1976. *The Relaxation Response*. New York: Harper Collins.

Bernhard, Gary and Kalman Glantz. 1992. *Staying Human in the Organization*. New York: Praeger.

Blumberg, Paul. 1980. *Inequality in an Age of Decline*. London: Oxford University Press.

Briggs, Jean L. 1970. *Never in Anger: Portrait of an Eskimo Family*. Cambridge: Harvard University Press.

Brinkmann, Svend. 2017. *Stand Firm: Resisting the Self-Improvement Craze*. Cambridge, UK: Polity Press.

Bronson, Sarah and Frans DeWaal. 2014, October 17. "Evolution of Responses to (Un)fairness." *Science*, 346.

Csikszentmihalyi, Mihaly. 1990. *Flow: The Psychology of Optimal Experience*. New York: Harper Perennial Modern Classics.

Filkins, Dexter. 2017, May 29. "The Warrior Monk." *New Yorker*.

Glantz, Kalman and Gary Bernhard. 2006. *Re-Uniting America*. EvoEbooks Online.

Glantz, Kalman and John Pearce. 1989. *Exiles From Eden: Psychotherapy From an Evolutionary Perspective*. New York: Norton.

Gordon, Thomas. 1977. *Leader Effectiveness Training*. New York: Wyden Books.

Heller, Zoë. 2017, April 10. "Where Prince Charles Went Wrong." *New Yorker*.

Herrigel, Eugen. 1953 (1999). *Zen in the Art of Archery*. New York: Vintage.

Junger, Sebastian. 2016. *Tribe: On Homecoming and Belonging*. New York: Hachette Book Group.

Kahneman, Daniel and Angus Deaton. 2010, September 21. "High Income Improves Evaluation of Life But Not Emotional Well-being." *PNAS*, 107(38): 16489–16493.

Kaplan, Helen Singer. 1974. *The New Sex Therapy*. New York: Brunner/Mazel.

Kernberg, Otto. 1975. *Borderline Conditions and Pathological Narcissism*. New York: Jason Aronson.

Kessler, David A. 2016. *Capture: Unraveling the Mystery of Mental Suffering*. New York: Harper Wave/HarperCollins.

Lee, Richard, and Irven DeVore, eds. 1968. *Man the Hunter*. New York: Aldine.

———. 1976. *Kalahari Hunter-Gatherers*. Cambridge: Harvard University Press.

Lemire, Christy. 2017, September 14. "Brads Status." www.rogerebert.com/reviews/brads-status-2017

106 References

Luthans, Fred. 1988. "Successful vs. Effective Real Managers." *Academy of Management Executive*, 2(2): 127–132.

Magnuson, Warren and Jean Carper. 1972. *The Dark Side of the Market Place.* Englewood Cliffs, NJ: Prentice Hall.

Marshall Thomas, Elizabeth. 1959. *The Harmless People.* New York: Vintage.

McKenna, Elizabeth Perl. 1997. *When Work Doesn't Work Anymore.* New York: Delacorte Press.

Northouse, Peter. 2016. *Leadership Theory and Practice.* 7th edition. Thousand Oaks, CA: SAGE.

O'Connor, Lynn et al. 2001. "Survivor Guilt, Submissive Behavior and Evolutionary Theory: The Down-side of Winning in Social Competition." *British Journal of Medical Psychology*, 73: 519–530.

Raeburn, Paul and Kevin Zollman. 2016. *The Game Theorist's Guide to Parenting.* New York: Scientific American/Farrar Straus & Giroux.

Ratey, John and Catherine Johnson. 1997. *Shadow Syndromes.* New York: Pantheon Books.

Sahlins, M. 1968. "Notes on the Original Affluent Society." In *Man the Hunter*, edited by R. Lee and I. DeVore. New York: Aldine.

Schwartz, Alexandra. 2016, May 23. "Work It: Is Dating Worth the Effort?" *New Yorker*.

Sengupta, Somini. 2016. *The End of Karma: Hope and Fury Among India's Young.* New York: Norton.

Shermer, Michael. 2008. *The Mind of the Market.* New York: Henry Holt & Co.

Shostak, Marjorie. 1981. *Nisa: The Life and Words of a !Kung Woman.* Cambridge: Harvard University Press.

Smith, Sally Bedel. 2017. *Prince Charles: The Passions and Paradoxes of an Improbable Life.* New York: Random House.

Tonkinson, Robert. 1978. *The Mardudjara Aborigines: Living the Dream in Australia's Desert.* New York: Holt, Rinehart and Winston.

Trivers, Robert. 1971, March. "The Evolution of Reciprocal Altruism." *The Quarterly Review of Biology*, 46(1): 35–57.

Turnbull, Colin M. 1961. *The Forest People.* New York: Simon and Schuster.

Upadhayaya, Venus. 2013, May 30. "An Untouchable-Caste Woman Forges Into Indian Village Politics." *Epoch Times*. www.theepochtimes.com/an-untouchable-caste-woman-forges-into-indian-politics_80813.html

Verhaeghe, Paul. 2014. *What About Me: The Struggle for Identity in a Market-Based Society.* Brunswick Victoria Australia: Scribe Publications.

Weber, Max. 2002. *The Protestant Ethic and the Spirit of Capitalism* (Trans. Peter Beher and Gordon Wells). New York: Penguin Books.

Weigel, Moira. 2016. *Labor of Love: The Invention of Dating.* New York: Farrar, Strauss & Giroux.

White, Mike. 2017, September 7. "Interview With Terri Gross." *Fresh Air*. www.npr.org/2017/09/07/548884881/director-mike-white-unpacks-the-impulse-to-compare-in-brad-s-status

Wood, Joanne V. et al. 2009. "Positive Self-Statements: Power for Some, Peril for Others." *Psychological Science*, 20(7): 860–866, Wiley Periodicals.